TO HELL AND BACK

The Story of Grimsby Town's 2017-2018 Football Season

Rob Sedgwick

To Hell and Back Copyright © 2018 by Rob Sedgwick. All Rights Reserved.

All rights reserved. No part of this book may be reproduced in any form or by any electronic or mechanical means including information storage and retrieval systems, without permission in writing from the author. The only exception is by a reviewer, who may quote short excerpts in a review.

Cover designed by Rob Sedgwick

The bulk of the contents of this book comprises posts from the independent Grimsby Town web site forum.thefishy.co.uk. Some of the posts have been changed to fix grammatical mistakes or in a few cases, words have been added to supply context.

Some of the messages in this book contain strong language. Do not read it if you are likely to be offended by such language.

Rob Sedgwick, Site Publisher
Visit our website at https://forum.thefishy.co.uk

This book is dedicated to the long-suffering supporters of Grimsby Town FC. Grimsby 'til we die.

Goals change football matches
—RUSSELL SLADE

'Tis better to have loved and lost than never to have loved at all
—ALFRED LORD TENNYSON

We piss on your fish
—GRIMSBY TOWN TERRACE CHANT

Contents

To Hell and Back 1
Preamble 5
Introduction 7
Dramatis Personæ 10
    Players 10
    Managers 12
    Board members (non-Supporters Trust) 12
    Supporters 12
    Posters 12
May 14
    Week 1 15
    Week 2 17
    Week 3 18
    Week 4 19
June 21
    Week 5 21
    Week 6 22
    Week 7 22
    Week 8 23
July 25
    Week 9 25
    Week 10 25
    Week 11 27
    Week 12 27
August 29
    Week 13 29
    Week 14 30
    Week 15 31
    Week 16 34
September 38
    Week 17 38
    Week 18 39
    Week 19 40

Week 20	43
Week 21	46
October	50
Week 22	50
Week 23	51
Week 24	53
Week 25	55
November	59
Week 26	59
Week 27	61
Week 28	65
Week 29	68
Week 30	70
December	74
Week 31	74
Week 32	76
Week 33	82
Week 34	83
January	88
Week 35	88
Week 36	90
Week 37	91
Week 38	93
Week 39	95
February	100
Week 39 (continued)	100
Week 40	103
Week 41	107
Week 42	112
Week 43	116
March	121
Week 43	121
Week 44	123
Week 45	127
Week 46	132

Week 47	137
Week 48	140
April	146
Week 48 (continued)	146
Week 49	151
Week 50	155
Week 51	160
Week 52	164
Conclusions	171
Aftermath	173
Acknowledgements	174

PREAMBLE

There is nothing like being there. Many football books are written long after the events described, when the passage of time has rounded stories to fit the facts and views altered by subsequent events.

This book is written in the words of Grimsby Town supporters. All the comments were written on the popular forum The Fishy. They were all written by supporters at the time, as they saw things, and without the benefit of hindsight. Many of the comments were written straight after the games, on the bus or train home, in the car, or even in one case in the collection, sat despairingly in the ground.

Quite often we humans get it wrong, especially when speculating about the future, and football fans are no exception. Frequently the memories we preserve do not actually portray the way we really felt, the despair we experienced, or the anger that coursed through our bodies. Time is a great changer of views and opinions, but this volume tries to capture what it was like to live through this year and follow the fortune of the Mariners, day by day, week by week.

The posts that have been selected are ones which were "liked" at the time by fellow readers. I am therefore assuming that the posts roughly struck a chord with how supporters felt *at the time*. There are many thousands of messages that were not selected, a lot of these are doubtless worthy contenders to appear in this volume, had they received enough green ticks. Sometimes, when the site is busy, a good post gets buried in a river of messages and does not receive the positive feedback it deserves, but I hope that the messages selected offer a fair insight into the views of the supporters, although doubtless a more thorough examination of the whole collection could unearth even finer jewels.

The aim of this book, therefore, is to offer a transcript of the season from contemporary sources which hopefully represents its story as told by the people to whom it matters most, the supporters.

I have corrected the grammar and typos of the original posts where necessary, but I have tried to preserve as closely as possible the essence of their meaning. Occasionally where a post was a reply to a previous message I have added a few words to make it more self-contained. But I have strived to keep my own footprint as light as possible, so the original meaning is preserved.

Rob Sedgwick

I have provided commentary to knit together the text into a coherent story. It will make the most sense to supporters of Grimsby Town, or at least those that follow the team closely. I hope it will be of interest to the more general reader, but I apologise if the thread is difficult to follow for those not intimately acquainted with the events described.

Above all, any mistakes are my own.

INTRODUCTION

The 2016-2017 season, Grimsby's first in the Football League following six years of being marooned in non-league, was in stark contrast to the years which immediately preceded it. At the end of the previous season in 2016, Town had won the National League play-offs at the fourth attempt. So, for four years, every game had been meaningful, initially in the quest to reach the top 5, and then try and get over the line into the promised land of the Football League, where Grimsby had spent the previous 100 years before they were relegated in 2010. Even the final years in the League in the late noughties had been predominantly been dominated by relegation battles. The one exception was in 2006 when Grimsby were within a minute of automatic promotion, only to concede a late goal to Northampton and end up losing to Cheltenham in the League One play-offs.

So, it was a shock to the system to find Town seemingly spend virtually the whole season in 14th place, despite having three different managers. After six years Paul Hurst left for Shrewsbury in October, capitalising on the name he'd made for himself getting promoted with Grimsby and his consistency in getting his teams into the play-offs. Marcus Bignot was enticed to Blundell Park from National League side Solihull Moors and sacked within 5 months – rumoured to be more for personal reasons then for football ones. Former Town boss Russell Slade was reappointed as Grimsby manager within a day of Bignot's departure despite having failed three times in quick succession at his former sides.

Grimsby never won more than two consecutive games in 2016-2017 and never lost more than three. Generally, win alternated draw alternated loss, to the extent that Grimsby were almost permanently 14th. There became little point in looking at any other results or working out what would happen if only a string of bad or good results would ensue. The reality was that Town seemed destined for mid-table mediocrity and predictably the team finished 14th. It was a change from the National League days when Grimsby had been one of the best-supported clubs and almost permanently near the top of the table under Paul Hurst's consistent stewardship, but it was a solid enough start in their first season back at this level.

As the chart below shows, Grimsby rarely left mid-table and spent virtually the whole of the second half of the season hovering around 14th place. They barely ever appeared in one of the play-off or relegation places.

2016 -2017 Week by Week

Town were never that many points away from the top 7 but finally ended 8 points and 7 places away from the promotion picture.

Pos	Team	P	W	D	L	F	A	GD	Pts
1	Portsmouth	46	26	9	11	79	40	+39	87
2	Plymouth	46	26	9	11	71	46	+25	87
3	Doncaster	46	25	10	11	85	55	+30	85
4	Luton	46	20	17	9	70	43	+27	77
5	Exeter	46	21	8	17	75	56	+19	71
6	Carlisle	46	18	17	11	69	68	+1	71
7	Blackpool	46	18	16	12	69	46	+23	70
8	Colchester	46	19	12	15	67	57	+10	69
9	Wycombe	46	19	12	15	58	53	+5	69
10	Stevenage	46	20	7	19	67	63	+4	67
11	Cambridge	46	19	9	18	58	50	+8	66
12	Mansfield	46	17	15	14	54	50	+4	66
13	Accrington	46	17	14	15	59	56	+3	65
14	Grimsby	46	17	11	18	59	63	-+4	62
15	Barnet	46	14	15	17	57	64	-+7	57
16	Notts County	46	16	8	22	54	76	-+22	56
17	Crewe	46	14	13	19	58	67	-+9	55
18	Morecambe	46	14	10	22	53	73	-+20	52
19	Crawley Town	46	13	12	21	53	71	-+18	51
20	Yeovil	46	11	17	18	49	64	-+15	50
21	Cheltenham	46	12	14	20	49	69	-+20	50
22	Newport County	46	12	12	22	51	73	-+22	48
23	Hartlepool	46	11	13	22	54	75	-+21	46
24	Leyton Orient	46	10	6	30	47	87	-+40	36

2016-2017 League Two Table

With Russell Slade in charge, nothing dramatic was expected to happen in the new season. Slade was deemed to be solid, but competent, something of a dinosaur playing negative football that produced enough positive results to keep him from getting the sack. Over the course of his 20+ year football management career, Slade had not managed to win a promotion. Although to be fair he'd come close a few times, though most of the "nearly" seasons were starting to be quite a few years ago. Most fans felt he was a safe pair of hands that would leave the club treading water until something better came along: a new ground, a new owner, anything really. The future looked, if not exciting, then at least solid.

Rob Sedgwick

DRAMATIS PERSONÆ

Players

Around 40 players were given squad numbers by Grimsby during the 2017-2018 Season. The number of appearances, including substitutions is shown. Grimsby played 51 games in total in all competitions.

1 James McKeown, Keeper (39 games)
First choice goalkeeper, the only remnant of the 2016 play-off winning side.
2 Ben Davies, Defender (37 games)
Right back at his 8th club
3 Paul Dixon, Defender (28 games)
Scottish international left back
4 Sean McAllister, Midfielder (2 games)
Central midfielder who had hardly played in his first season due to injury.
5 Nathan Clarke, Defender (48 games)
Central defender who had spent most of his career at Huddersfield
6 Danny Collins, Defender (44 games)
Former Welsh international central defender now in the second half of his thirties
7 James Berrett, Midfielder (34 games)
Central midfielder at his fifth club.
8 Mitch Rose, Midfielder (36 games)
Young central midfielder who had had spells at Mansfield and Newport
9 J J Hooper, Striker (35 games)
Young striker signed from Port Vale
10 Sam Jones, Striker (27 games)
Striker signed from Gateshead
10 Gary McSheffrey, Striker (6 games)
Veteran striker signed as a free agent
11 Sam Kelly, Midfielder (12 games)
Irish winger signed from Port Vale

12   **Zak Mills, Defender** (32 games)
Right back in his mid-20s at his third club
14   **Karleigh Osborne, Defender** (13 games)
Central defender who'd had lots of clubs but rarely played for any of them.
15   **Harry Clifton, Midfielder** (13 games)
Product of the Grimsby Youth system
16   **Jamey Osborne, Midfielder** (3 games)
Central midfielder who'd been first choice the previous season
16   **Easah Suliman, Defender** (2 games)
Central defender on loan from Aston Villa
17   **Harry Cardwell, Striker** (21 games)
Young striker from Hull who made his league debut with Town
18   **Tom Bolarinwa, Midfielder** (6 games)
Exciting winger brought from non-league
18   **Mallik Wilks, Striker** (6 games)
On-loan Leeds striker
19   **Luke Summerfield, Midfielder** (41 games)
Central midfielder at his fourth club
20   **Diallang Jaisyemi, Midfielder** (35 games)
Winger on loan from Norwich
21   **Scott Vernon, Striker** (30 games)
Veteran striker at his sixth club
22   **Chris Clements, Midfielder** (0 games)
Central midfielder who'd impressed during the previous season
23   **Akwasi Asante, Striker** (0 games)
Dutch-born striker brought from non-league
23   **Andrew Fox, Defender** (10 games)
Full back who'd last played in the Swedish Allsvenskan
24   **Jack Keeble, Defender** (0 games)
Youth team defender
25   **Martyn Woolford, Midfielder** (33 games)
Veteran winger at his eighth club
26   **Tom Sawyer, Midfielder** (0 games)
Youth team midfielder
27   **Siriki Dembele, Midfielder** (39 games)
Ivorian winger signed from the Nike Football Academy
28   **Ahkeem Rose, Striker** (0 games)
Jamaican striker unable to play due to lack of a work permit
29   **Jamille Matt, Striker** (36 games)
Striker on loan from Blackpool who had impressed against Town in non-league

30   Ben Killip, Keeper (10 games)
Young reserve keeper who spent Youth period at Norwich
31   Reece Hall-Johnson, Defender   12 games
Young defender brought from non-league
33   Jake Kean, Keeper (3 games)
Keeper on loan from Sheff Wed
34   Charles Vernam, Striker (9 games)
Striker on loan from Derby
39   Simeon Jackson, Striker (5 games)
Striker on loan from Walsall
41   Emil Powles, Defender (0 games)
Youth team defender

Managers

Russell Slade (Appointed late in the previous season and continued until February, commonly abbreviated to RS)
Paul Wilkinson (Assistant Manager with a spell as Caretaker)
Michael Jolley (from March until the end of the season)

Board members (non-Supporters Trust)

John Fenty (commonly abbreviated to JF)
Stephen Marley
Philip Day
Michael Chapman

Supporters

Grimsby's home crowds numbered between 3000 and 7000, with a few thousand "exiles" who attended at least one game away from Blundell Park (commonly abbreviated to BP). It's fair to say that the total number of people who actively support Grimsby Town, by attending at least one game per season, is well above ten thousand.

Posters

Around 700 different people posted on the Fishy during the 52 weeks of 2017-2018, including the preceding summer, and there were many more "lurkers" who regularly read the site but never contributed. Just under 100,000 messages appeared on the site during the period covered in this book, of which only a tiny selection made it into these pages.

MAY

The Beginning of the Beginning

May is the time of year when optimism can start again, and all of the previous campaign's mistakes are to be righted. With so many players retained it was not expected to be as busy as the previous summer when former boss Paul Hurst had recruited virtually an entire team.

In the end, the retained list was as follows:

Released: Craig Disley, Josh Gowling, Dan Jones, Ashley Chambers and Gavin Gunning, although club captain Craig Disley was granted a testimonial benefit game, for FA regulatory reasons.
Offers: Danny Andrew
Negotiations: Danny Collins, Shaun Pearson, Ben Davies, Max Wright, Josh Venney
Under contract: James McKeown, Andrew Boyce, Zak Mills, James Berrett, Chris Clements, Harry Clifton, Sam Jones, Sean McAllister, Jamey Osborne, Luke Summerfield, Tom Bolarinwa, Rhys Browne, Akwasi Asante, Adi Yussuf, Scott Vernon, Harry Clifton

WEEK 1

The club's owner John Fenty (aka JF), a perennial scapegoat for all ills past and present, was an early recipient of some pre-season goodwill.

JMT: Can I honestly say how much of a nice bloke John Fenty is?

I decided to ask for an interview on a documentary I was doing about the club, messaged him on the Fishy and got a reply the same day with his e-mail asking to forward him times.

After numerous exchanges of e-mails, we settled on the day, which was today. He suggested the place we film this interview was his house.

I must say for all the criticism John gets, he is probably one of the friendliest blokes I have had the pleasure of meeting. As soon as we entered his house, he straight away offered us a drink and told me and my partner to make ourselves at home whilst setting up the camera. During the interview, he didn't hesitate to any questions and gave honest answers.

I can't speak highly enough of him now, everything from Monday to today has been an absolute breeze.

He has helped a college student complete his documentary and gained a lot of respect from me.

I would just like to say thank you, John.

__Skrill:__ In the era when clubs are abundant with chairmen that conduct shady behind-the-scenes activities, non-appearance, and spoilt arrogance, I think some people need to realise how lucky we are to have a partly fan-owned club, with an open de facto chairman.

__1mickylyons:__ I had a disagreement with him a few years back and wasn't his biggest fan but he asked if he could call me and I agreed. I have to say he was very honest and gave a lot of time to the call. He wears his heart on his sleeve and that causes him to make a few gaffes but he has stuck it out when most would have walked. Fair play for that. Whilst I don't always agree with him and sometimes he really annoys me in the press he does 101 other things that are positive and he gets zero credit. A touch of class regarding Disley, to me that's what Fenty is all about.

Meanwhile, on a national level, the much-despised Checkatrade Trophy continued to be targeted by fans as a tournament to be boycotted at all costs in the new season. This had caused a divide between the board and many of the fans after it came to light that the directors under the leadership of John Fenty, had voted for the new format of the Checkatrade Trophy (which included Premier League U-23 sides). Their reasons were primarily financial, although they assured fans that there was no prospect of any Premier League "B" teams ever being allowed in the Football League, which is what many supporters believed this was the first step towards.

RichMariner: *I've had enough of Shaun Harvey, B-teams, League 3 and all that other nonsense the EFL try and peddle to suit the PL.*

We should use one of their Checkatrade Trophy matches to set a new record-low attendance at BP.

Not just a boycott.

A proper campaign; an operation, if you like, with a name. We're bloody brilliant at those.

Whatever U-23 team we play at BP, we use that fixture to see how low we can get our attendance.

In fact, why don't we organise a fans' match on the same night and see if we can get more people to attend that than BP?

That would make an incredible news story and be a powerful message to Harvey.

We're so pissed off with you lot, that we've just created our own match and it's more popular than your competition.

Any other ideas of how we can tell the EFL to shove their Checkatrade monstrosity?

WEEK 2

This week saw the news that long-standing defender Shaun Pearson had been allowed by Russell Slade to leave. Pearson was one of a handful of players still left from the team which won at Wembley, only a year before. With very little known at this stage about who was to replace Pearson, it was difficult to be too critical.

Civvy at last: We were always going to have players leaving that for various reasons we would like to have kept. But let's wait and see who comes in as well before we moan.

Personally, I believe Shaun could most definitely have played a big role for us next season. But I am not privy to what he wanted, or what we offered. I also (for a change) don't blame the GTFC PR department (if such a thing actually exists).

Shaun's statement (I believe) was unfortunately worded. No formal contract may have been offered. But this was probably due to the fact that negotiations had reached the point of no return. It doesn't mean he was always going to be released. At the moment I am disappointed the way things are going.

But until I see the starting squad for next season I'm keeping my hands off the panic button. UTM

ginnywings: The squad we have are good enough to hold their own in League 2, but to progress, we need players capable of getting out of this league and holding their own in the one above. Players come and go and some we get more emotionally attached to than others; Shaun being one of them. I felt that he was 50-50 to be here next year because no doubt he is good enough to play at this level and is a great servant, but is he good enough to take us to the next level? Some will say he is and that's fair enough, but the manager has to look at it impartially and from a purely footballing perspective. I'd be happy if he stays, but I won't be heartbroken if he moves on. It's football and it's the name of the game. If the manager feels he can do better, then we have to back his decision.

BP Vicar: A shambolic decision, I am gutted to lose Shaun. He should have taken the armband for me, he's 27, coming into his prime. I felt he improved last season and would have been a key player next season.

Bigdog: The character and service of Shaun Pearson will be sorely missed. A great servant and a genuine top, top bloke.

In his interview, he came across as being far more pragmatic than a lot of GTFC fans.

Dis and Shaun are admired by all, but this admiration clouds fans' opinions on their footballing ability. Look at where they are going to play next season, Alfreton and Wrexham. If they were confident of getting better deals, they would not have signed this early. They have both assessed they could not gamble on getting better two-year deals elsewhere, so why would we sign them for a promotion push when they feel every other club in League Two wouldn't give them a deal?

It was clear to see how slow our team was in comparison to other teams in League Two. From the two new signings, it's also clear to see that RS is addressing this already.

It is heartbreaking to see two incredibly well-loved and respected professionals leave our club in a matter of days. We'll all follow them from afar as we should, but I think we need to be as pragmatic as Shaun has been and look forward to the new season with an open heart and start to let one or two new potential legends in.

WEEK 3

With the new season a long way away, and no summer tournaments (it being an odd-numbered year), fans were at least wondering why they couldn't buy a season ticket for the season to come, and why the signings were so slow to arrive.

Scrumble: *No football on, so we really have to scrape the bottom of the barrel to find something to whinge about. The season finished what, three weeks ago? The season won't start for over two months. How is it taking the piss to not have tickets for sale?*

As for announcing players, there are all sorts of reasons for not making it public straight away, and not necessarily because of GTFC. The usual is simply down to when his contract expires at the player's former club. You can hardly announce a new player when he still belongs to another team for another few weeks.

Chrisblor: *Ours aren't even on sale yet because the club is incapable of forward planning or any kind of innovative marketing. Hope this helps!*

Diehardmariner: I think that's very harsh. The club could well have ordered some season ticket books as early as February/March time but what would have happened if the club changed name or the two years that the season fall in changed, or even what if the alphabet changed and all the letters for each stub had to be changed? We would have looked very foolish!

Meanwhile, the first new signing arrived, Mitch Rose from Newport. Fans, many without much knowledge of the players, as ever looked at numbers to see if their new signings were any good.

grimsby pete: Rose played in 35 games in all last season for Mansfield and Newport. He was suspended for 5 games so he did not miss many games when he was not suspended. So two different managers played him most of the time.

WEEK 4

The next player to arrive was Sam Kelly, an Irish winger from newly relegated Port Vale, who apparently was not highly regarded by some at Vale Park

TheRonRaffertyFanClub: Two or three thoughts:-

One, he's been in L1 and we are in L2 so at his age I would expect he has some ability to show us.

Two, he is unknown to us but a known quantity to the management, so they will have a plan in mind that he will fit into and will use his strengths.

Three, if he throws a wobbler or doesn't cut the mustard he will not last long in a Slade team.

BottesfordMariner: I shall wait to pass judgement until I have actually seen him play in a GTFC shirt. I am not bothered what some Vale fans think tbh.

I have seen players arrive at BP with big expectations and they have failed to live up to them and others who have arrived under the radar so to speak and turned out to be pretty good signings.

Sometimes a player arrives at a new club and it just clicks with the coach/manager who gets the best of them. They move on and sometimes it just isn't the same. Let's hope Slade & Wilkinson can bring out the best in him.

I like his age along with experience and he looks to have some ability and could help us in our attacking play. Our signings already look like they have added some athleticism and dynamism to the team.

ginnywings: In his interview, he said he had offers from League 1 but wanted to work with Slade and Wilko, who he knows from Norwich.

I await the "he's shit because Port Vale fans say so" type posts.

'Allo 'Allo Sam. :)

sam gy: We sign a player who has played in the leagues above us and it's still not good enough. Honestly, I don't know what people expect.

JUNE

The Quiet Month

WEEK 5

With no new signings, fans looked at the existing squad members still on the books.

Jimgtfc: Berrett and Summerfield different players in my opinion. Summerfield likes to be an all-action central midfielder who wins challenges and sprays the ball about. He's got a decent engine on him and he can do the box to box role well enough. His downfall is his decision making. When he gives the ball away he does it in style and it has lead to goals being conceded.

Berrett is more of a utility player for me. A bit of a poor man's James Milner. He can do a job anywhere across the midfield or we've seen him play behind the striker. He's not blessed with pace or trickery, but he holds the ball well, gives it simple and has good positional sense helping the team retain shape.

I'd not be averse to either player being part of our squad next season as I don't think either player is anywhere near as bad as people make out. But if we want to be progressing towards a promotion team then maybe we need better.

Plus, the frustration of little happening, had some wondering whether the club was doing enough to sell itself.

Bigdog: Season ticket sales probably account for a third of the club's income every season. As it's such a significant part, I find the marketing around it extremely half-hearted and uninspiring. It could be looked at cynically and be judged at taking our loyal fans for granted or even the club *giving up on attracting the floating fan. It could even be a lack of effort, lack of expertise or just a case of managing the status quo until the new stadium appears. I just don't understand it.*

I know a lot of fans on here will renew theirs without question and wonder what all the fuss is about, but it isn't about them, it's about putting forward such an attractive offer that not only all of the loyal renew, but the not so loyal are tempted too. Looking around at how a lot of other clubs have been pro-active, all I can say from a marketing point of view, it's been a pretty poor show, especially when the club have put together the odd piece of decent PR from time to time over the past year or two.

WEEK 6

Meanwhile newly promoted Lincoln had not followed in Grimsby's footsteps of offloading most of their promotion-winning squad, and the season ticket sales at Sincil Bank were going through the roof after the title-winning season and FA Cup run.

OllieGTFC: *Can we stop going on about fucking Lincoln, none of us cares. Let them sell 5,000 season tickets it doesn't mean anything, I thought we were all Town, aren't we?*

Hagrid *(replying to another poster): nothing against you Grim but who cares about the Gimps?! Let them do what they need to do and let's focus on GTFC - we've only made 3 [signings].*

WEEK 7

There were still no signings and fans were hoping this was a sign that the management team were biding their time finding quality players.

Mariner93er: *Or maybe most people have the foresight to see that the season is over a month away, and signing the first bloke that comes available isn't the best option.*

sam gy: *Oh dear, we're already going to have a shit season and the manager is already getting stick, despite NOBODY having a clue what our first 11 will even look like on the opening day, which is ages away. I feel like I've said this before, but has the Fishy sunk to a new low?*

Meanwhile, of the existing squad, hopes were resting on the injury-prone Akwasi Asante making an impression in the new season.

Grimreaper: *Akwasi had a successful operation a few weeks ago. He is now walking unaided and without a cast.*

He has been in the gym every day this week, and on Monday is spending a week or possibly two weeks at St Georges Park to receive intensive training and physiotherapy.

He is looking good and cannot wait to get back to football fully fit which he has not been for a couple of years.

I would predict that he should be near to fitness and possibly on the bench by the start of the third week in August.

Fingers crossed

WEEK 8

The news that Spurs and Man City were to enter the Checkatrade Trophy was not greeted with much enthusiasm.

diehardmariner: *Only one solution to this - total boycott.*

Some hoped that Padraig Amond might return to Town after he handed in a transfer request at Hartlepool. He was to eventually return to League 2, but it was to be at Newport, not Town.

headingly_mariner. *I don't think we have had a better goal scorer in the last 10 years. He shouldn't have been allowed to go and managed a decent return in a relegated side. He is easily capable of 20+ in a decent side.*

OllieGTFC. *He has handed a transfer request. He clearly doesn't want to be in non-league again, he should have never have left.*

Meanwhile, Town fans were thinking of the Mariners whilst on holiday.

MarinerRob. *After leaving Pigeon Forge, Tennessee on my coaster holiday I drove across the Smokey Mountains and stayed at Cherokee, North Carolina. The intention was to ride the Rudi Coaster at Santa's Land. Combining with my other interest of Grimsby Town football I wore my Grimsby shirt. It appears that I am only the second person from the UK to ride this coaster according to Coaster Count.*

Thinking about it - it was very strange to be riding a Rudolph themed coaster in the middle of the Smokey Mountains in June with temperatures in the high nineties wearing a Grimsby Town shirt. Clearly being a 'pensioner' has affected my brain.

JULY

Pre-season begins

WEEK 9

Mid-season optimism was blooming in some quarters:

Stew0_0: *I think this squad is going to surprise us this season as players like Jones and Osborne have league experience now and a full-time pre-season. All the players look leaner and fitter and I am happy with the new additions.*

The key will be how we recruit up front and that will be the difference between us challenging for promotion or another comfortable mid-table finish.

I am confident Slade can still bring in 2/3 more gems yet

WEEK 10

The first serious pre-season friendly saw Grimsby beat Scunthorpe 4-0 at Blundell Park. Fans were understandably buzzing.

ginnywings: *A pleasant stroll in the sun and an enjoyable game, if a tad one-sided. I had to laugh at the sign outside BP Hotel saying home supporters only. Good amount in the ground, certainly more than for most reserve games. So...*

Scunny were very young and inexperienced and one or two of them looked about 14 years old. Subsequently, our defence was totally untroubled, so it's hard to say much about Dixon. He was not bothered at all defensively and not a lot to report going forward, but what he did do was tidy and he looks to be a steady Eddy with a decent cross in his locker. He mis-controlled a couple of opportunities but worth another look. Wilko had a long chat with him when he came off, so make of that what you will.

The Gowling lookalike was tall, elegant, languid and very economical. He did a lot of first-time passes and sprayed some lovely balls out wide. He didn't try too hard and just coasted around the pitch. You could tell he has played at a higher level but there were 2 things about him I noticed. No left foot at all and played as many passes with the outside of his right foot as he did with the instep. He also got caught in possession more than once but that could be down to playing in leagues where they get more time and space. If signed, could be anything from a revelation to a liability, perhaps in the same game.

Paul Jones didn't get long enough to do much of note, so can't say much about him. The other trialist Rollins looked quick and strong but again not a lot of time to assess.

Best trialist for me was Robinson. Quick, strong and tricky. Played right from one side to the other, put in some wicked crosses, one of which Yussuf scored from and rifled in a cracking goal too. Worth another look definitely for me.

Of the others, it was the first time I've seen Dembele and Cardwell. The former is very quick with equally quick feet and surprisingly strong for his size. Cardwell is a lot bigger than I imagined and looks a decent player. He scored a good goal, then fluffed a simple chance but I think he's also worth another look against stronger opposition. Bolarinwa was very disappointing, given the strength of the Scunny players and given his pace and power. He didn't do much at all. Summerfield was neat and tidy but nothing more. Yussuf looks very fit, strong and athletic and to me looks improved on last season. He could be a useful player next year.

Right, need to get back in my workshop now.

WEEK 11

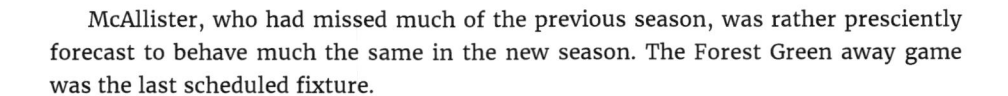

McAllister, who had missed much of the previous season, was rather presciently forecast to behave much the same in the new season. The Forest Green away game was the last scheduled fixture.

***Abdul19**: McAllister will be like a new signing when he returns for the Forest Green away game.*

WEEK 12

News that the Club had banned the local newspaper the Cleethorpes Chronicle from interviewing Grimsby manager Russell Slade did not go down well. This wasn't the first time that local media had been punished for some perceived misdemeanour.

***Chrisblor**: Is this a new low? Absolutely shameful stuff from the club - we really are run by a bunch of clowns. Fenty and his useless mate in charge of Press and PR (Dale Ladson) really need some competent replacements who actually understand the value of local journalism, especially considering they'll need all the support they can get if they ever want this new stadium built.*

Meanwhile, the enigmatic Adi Yussuf was still being touted by some fans as one to look out for in the coming campaign.

***Perkins** (when asked what he saw in Yussuf): WHY? Because he's ours, because he's talented, because he's got more bottle than most other kids of his age I've seen at BP for years, he was told by RS to show him what he could do to earn a contract, he's played in nearly every position but his own so far and never let himself or anyone down, he's certainly shown he's worth a deal as far as I'm concerned. Probably only a bencher this season but worth a deal. ...*

That's why.

AUGUST

The Season Starts

WEEK 13

Town won the opening game against Chesterfield 3-1, an away win against a side who had been in League One last year. It looked a good result and was a very promising start to the campaign. The only downside came in a late sending off for Zak Mills.

GTFC Garner: Just home, what a great away performance. I believe that Chesterfield were the better footballing team no doubt but we had more grit, determination and the right attitude. What do you say to your players at half-time when you're 2-0 up against a team who are heavily tipped for promotion? Second half we soaked up the pressure excellently and it was a great finish by Denniss to make it 2-1 but we came straight back. The defenders looked solid all game, won a gritty away game which may prove absolutely vital come the end of the season. Going home so happy UTFM

LH: Vernon is an absolute workhorse and is unfairly criticised because he won't get loads of goals. You need players like that in a squad over a season.

A Brace Of Tees: If that's "the Slade way" then I'm all for it...it sounds perfect! I just wish his predecessor had just 10% of Slade's organisational skills and tactical understanding, then we might not have seen last season dwindle away to nothing.

Striker JJ Hooper, after a long trial at BP, finally signed for Town AFTER the opening game against Chesterfield and was presented with the No 9 Jersey. It had taken all summer and overrun by one game, but Town had finally completed their squad (or at least the pre-assigned shirt numbers).

Mighty Mariner: *In terms of JJ Hooper... No idea if he's any good or not but I'd sign him for this reason alone (quotes from Wikipedia):*

"Hooper had trials at Scottish sides Dunfermline Athletic, Inverness Caledonian Thistle and Raith Rovers in summer 2015, before playing two friendlies for Cheltenham Town. He impressed enough to win a contract with the club and was photographed with manager Gary Johnson when he was informed of interest from League One club Port Vale; Hooper sneaked out of Whaddon Road to speak with Port Vale shortly before he was due to sign a contract with Cheltenham. The Cheltenham club website initially reported that Hooper had signed a one-year contract. In August 2015, he was revealed as a Port Vale player after signing a two-year contract with the club".

What a lad! We all like a good story where Cheltenham are screwed over :) :)

WEEK 14

A week later and Town lost 2-0 at home in their first match at Blundell Park, with Berrett being sent off late in the game. It was against fancied Coventry, another relegated side though, so the defeat was tinged with some realism, especially as Grimsby had a player sent off for the second game running.

---

ginnywings: *We did nothing, created nothing, deserved nothing and got nothing. Sladeball is alive and well and at BP.*

It could be a long season if that is the way we are going to play and we will probably have more joy away from home than at home, which is pretty much what happened last time Slade was here. I wasn't a fan then and I'm not a fan now. Hitting the corners at every opportunity and mostly losing possession in the process. The two best players were Jones and Dembele. Unfortunately, Jones had way more of the ball than Dembele, who watched the ball constantly fly over his head. The only time he got it to feet, he looked very dangerous, but that was all too brief. Apart from a couple of Jones shots over the bar, we didn't have a serious shot at their keeper.

It's hard to say at this early stage how good Coventry are, but they were well worth the points and could be heading straight back up, so it's hard to judge if we were just not good enough on the day, or we not good enough full stop.

I am getting fairly cheesed off with our poor home form going back for seasons now and today doesn't fill me great hope for the rest of the season. We're too disjointed, gave away possession cheaply time and again, and gave our obligatory gift goal. Much improvement is needed if we are to challenge at the top end. Managers come and go, players come and go, but the erratic home form persists. I don't mind losing games but at least give us something to cheer about. Not a lot to get you out of your seat today and I hope it's just down to a slow start.

LondonMariner43: Probably an unpopular view but considering the unbalanced squad RS inherited, he's done a pretty good job of bringing in some decent players and getting some balance into the squad. When everyone is fit and firing it looks much better than a year ago.

WEEK 15

Disappointment continued after the defeat by Coventry with another setback against Stevenage. This time though it was a more emphatic defeat, and Town had yet another player sent off, making it three games out of three. The fans continued to blame Russell Slade.

TheCodfather1966: I am not surprised at all by the last couple of performances by Town. The reality is that we did not strengthen our team at all in the summer months, all we did was bide our time to see which dregs were still floating about without a club and then offered them a deal, predominantly because no other clubs came in for them. You certainly get what you pay for in players and managers alike, and a season of consolidation/survival awaits us. It's very early days and I certainly back the managers fully, I somehow don't so much blame the management team, as much as the Board for the complete lack of backing the managers seem to have had in the transfer market. That said, Slade does need to get some better style of play going in the next few games if possible. We have relatively poor players at the club now, one thing is for sure, they all need to give 100% every game because what they clearly lack in ability, they need to make up for in effort. A long season ahead, and a tough one methinks.

Swansea_Mariner: *I honestly don't think he's been short-changed, he signed 10 new players and got all the backroom staff the last two managers were practically begging for.*

The Old Codger: *He could sign 100 new players but beyond Dembele, do you see anyone that has improved us? Clarke & Dixon are worse than Pearson & Andrew, Kelly is worse than Berrett & Summerfield, Hooper is worse than Yussuf.*

Meanwhile, fans were in uproar after Stevenage, in which fans were extensively searched including (most notoriously) female supporters who were asked to lift up their bras.

---

pontoonlew: *Not sure where to start, an absolutely disgraceful performance, gross treatment of the fans by the stewards as well.*

Hooper was a fucking joke, as was his other Port Vale counterpart. Not even sure where to start with everybody else, a circus from front to back.

Thoughts were already turning on what to do in what remained of the transfer window, still with a few days to go.

Bigdog *(replying to a suggestion that it would "cost a fortune" to replace the players already at the club): I don't expect a big turnaround from the powers that be but we need one.*

What will cost a fortune is 1k dropping off the home gate. £15k x 20 odd [games left] = £300k

Alternatively: we loan three out and pay half their wages, say 3x 25k = £75k

Sign three quality players £75k a year =£225k

In effect, the total cost is zero the way it's going.

Sitting on our hands and dropping out of the league could cost us £600k per annum at this rate.

What I don't understand is we have similar to or better than home receipts compared to 70% of all clubs in League One and League Two, League One clubs receiving only £200k more from the EFL which only equates to 5% of turnover, yet we act like clubs like Accrington, Newport or Morecambe who live on gates of less than 2k. Something's wrong somewhere.

What's the alternative? Wring our effing hands and hope for the best?

And Mariner09.. We were told the January signings were funded from unexpectedly high gate receipts, not the Bogle money, so it should still be there.

God help anyone sticking their neck out in the boardroom to get the fans hopeful and excited for once. We back this club through thick and thin and are expected to put up with the same old crap season after season. Dover have got a bigger budget etc etc etc.

It's nearly two decades since any serious money was invested in the club, this needs to change. It feels to me that the fans like the poor buggers that travelled today are taken for granted. The only excitement for years was generated by the fans themselves, no one else has done so.

I thought RS had enough about him to whip JF into shape. I haven't seen any evidence of that yet or little evidence of RS and PW extensive contacts and recruiting skills.

As you can tell, I'm a little fed up of narrow-minded thinking. ITV Digital collapse was 15 years ago, 15 years is a long time to be following a club that quite frankly never has any new ideas, never mind running out of them.

The Supporters Trust reacted very rapidly to events on the ground and within hours put out a superb letter to Stevenage http://www.marinerstrust.co.uk/mariners-trust-letter-to-stevenage-f-c/. This was widely picked up and reported by the national press.

Stevenage henceforth was known as "Bragate" and featured heavily in the national press, for example in *The Mirror*: http://google.com/newsstand/s/CBIwvNfz9jk.

---

crusty ole pie: *A great letter well done the Trust if a reasonable response is not received I suggest the Trust organise a total boycott of this fixture next year. I am not sure how many we took yesterday but a possible 1000 fans paying £21 - can a club really afford to lose £21000 in gate revenue?*

WEEK 16

Attention turned on the club after a lukewarm response to the events at Stevenage. Although the Supporters Trust's response was thorough and rapid, the club's effort said very little.

Barralad: *The Stevenage reply is a flagrant attempt to put the blame on GTFC. Fortunately, the SLO had kept a record of the communication she'd had with Stevenage and on the same night GTFC put out a statement refuting Stevenage's view and fully supporting the stance taken by The Trust.*

The SLO has handled herself with a great deal of dignity in a very pressurised situation.

marinernige *The anger at the treatment of genuine law-abiding Town fans has been building for some time now and Stevenage was the straw that broke the camel's back. We're all sick of being treat like hooligans/2nd class citizens. It's also time the club started acknowledging the fact that the overwhelming majority of us are well-behaved folks who just want to follow the club we love.*

Grimsby continued their remarkable streak of having a player sent off in every game. Town lost 1-0 in the EFL Cup at Blundell Park to Derby (Ben Davies red card) and 3-2 at home to Wycombe in the league (Danny Collins was sent off). It wasn't just the lack of results and the red cards that were bothering the fans, it was the long-term strategy of the club.

Bigdog: *Fans are starting to vote with their feet [following 4017 in the home game with Wycombe]. Home league gates are dropping and it's only the second one of the season. Negative board, negative manager, negative signings, negative football and if we're going to be the best part of £15k down per game because of this, the money is not going to be there to sort it out.*

Fenty has never been a speculate-to-accumulate chairman. We need someone to help push us forward, provide some excitement, not someone who works out a worst-case scenario for the season and sets the budget from there. What happens is eventually you get the worst-case scenario and if we drop out of the league again, I don't think we'll be back any time soon.

JF, you need to go out and find people to help you, because what you do just does not work. GTFC is not your plaything for life because you chucked in a few quid nearly two decades ago, it's ours. But, I can just picture you in an empty BP in a few years time with Town playing Clee Town in the Conference North still believing your way is best.

chaos33: *Fenty and Slade have killed it [The 2 Year plan]. End of. A big following desperate to get behind a promotion bid, and they try to do it on the cheap and get found out. You watch the fans go "no thanks" and walk away. A player sent off every game?! Losing at home to average teams?! A load of crap.*

The club then enraged supports by prioritising Mansfield away tickets to non-season ticket holders possessing ticket stubs for a Checkatrade game against Doncaster at Blundell Park, a match most fans were intent on boycotting.

Bigdog: *It is a cynical and disrespectful move by JF and the club. It makes his statement in the summer about understanding the feelings of the fans about this farce of a tournament no more than lip service. It proves that the divide between the club and fans is just getting wider.*

Just remember this when you're about to type that you'd rather a fan of GTFC run the club rather than anyone else. Andrea Radrizzani is not a lifelong fan of Leeds United, but since he took over the club in the summer, he has galvanised the whole city behind him. He gets Leeds so much more than JF gets GTFC, and that's in three months.

JF has been in charge for a very long time now and looks like he's going to be in charge for the rest of my lifetime. The Checkatrade farce and the way he uses the Trust, it smacks of a mini-dictatorship. We need a fresh start and a leader who the fans feel are on their side just like Radrizzani.

Yes I know, JF stuck his £2-3m in to save the club, but that's a hell of a long time ago. He still owns that figure in share value and should recoup that figure in any sale. For that kind of money, I think 15 years is about long enough to call the shots at a football club in this day and age. I don't think the figure he's put in gives him the moral right to be in charge for as long as he sees fit. It could be another twenty or thirty years of our club being run the JF way. Does that fill anyone with an iota of excitement? I'm sure JF does the best he can, but is it good enough any more? And is it right for one man to shape a community's football club in his own vision over several generations long of supporters for a couple of million quid which is dwarfed by the fans' contribution to the club over that period?

All these years later, he still acts like it's us and them and this decision regarding ticket stubs just proves it. We deserve better than this and we need to be pushing for change. I've spent a couple of decades being frustrated, not entertained or excited watching my club, feeding on scraps and the thought of twenty more years of this fills me with dread.

We desperately need new investment and thinking at the club, and if JF loved the club more than running it, he should be out there trying to bring fresh cash and blood in and have the good grace to loosen his stranglehold. If he did that, I'd thank him for his efforts and for saving my club. I know it's the Grimsby way to question who, why, what and where, change could be a negative step and all that. But why are we always so fearful of change and so inward looking? Do we always have to be so, well, Grimsby?

I will never fall out of love with GTFC but I'm seriously running out of patience with a club that never gives me any encouragement to retain that spark. I need it to give me something back rather than it just relying on my loyalty because it knows I'll always be there, one of the hundred or so who went to Carlisle midweek after the Auto Windscreens final in '98 or travelling twice in a week to Colchester after the first one was waterlogged.

Checkatrade ticket stub bribe for away tickets. FFS

Grimsby lost the EFL Trophy game to Doncaster, not that many fans cared as only 862 attended the game, but Town did at least finish the game with 11 men on the pitch for the first time this season.

The league table did not make pretty reading with just 1 win in 5 games which saw the Mariners perched just about the bottom two. It was certainly not the start many had hoped for after the win at Chesterfield.

Pos	Team	P	W	D	L	F	A	GD	Pts
1	Exeter	4	3	1	0	7	4	+3	10
2	Newport County	4	2	2	0	9	5	+4	8
3	Stevenage	4	2	2	0	8	5	+3	8
4	Crewe	4	2	2	0	5	3	+2	8
5	Luton	4	2	1	1	13	5	+8	7
6	Accrington	4	2	1	1	9	7	+2	7
7	Notts County	4	2	1	1	8	7	+1	7
8	Wycombe	4	2	1	1	10	10	0	7
9	Swindon	4	2	1	1	4	5	-1	7
10	Coventry	4	2	0	2	5	3	+2	6
11	Carlisle	4	2	0	2	7	7	0	6
12	Yeovil	4	2	0	2	10	14	-4	6
13	Lincoln	4	1	2	1	7	5	+2	5
14	Mansfield	4	1	2	1	7	6	+1	5
15	Morecambe	4	1	2	1	3	3	0	5
16	Colchester	4	1	1	2	7	8	-1	4
17	Barnet	4	1	1	2	3	4	-1	4
18	Cambridge	4	1	1	2	2	3	-1	4
19	Forest Green	4	1	1	2	7	12	-5	4
20	Crawley Town	4	1	0	3	4	5	-1	3
21	Port Vale	4	1	0	3	5	7	-2	3
22	Grimsby	4	1	0	3	6	9	-3	3
23	Cheltenham	4	1	0	3	5	9	-4	3
24	Chesterfield	4	1	0	3	4	9	-5	3

League Table 31st August

SEPTEMBER

Consistently Inconsistent

WEEK 17

Town beat Crewe 1-0 in the first game of September to get the season back on track after three consecutive defeats, and two cup losses.

ginnywings: *Much better. For the first home game this season, we didn't look second best and deservedly won. I thought Osborne had a great full debut at the back and the others in defence were solid too. Woolford looked a little off the pace but you can tell he's a decent player. Reports of Hooper's shiteness are greatly exaggerated, I thought he had a good solid game, but for me, the MOTM was the goalscorer Rose, who I thought had an excellent game. He puts out a lot of fires and always seems to be where the ball is, which is a good sign in a player.*

Vernon made us tick much better up front and he is a very clever footballer. He was missed in his absence. Dembele had some good moments but the end product isn't there from him yet. Matt looked a handful for their tiring defence and looks to be a decent change striker.

All round, it was much more balanced and with a better game plan. I'm not sure if Crewe were average or we made them look average, but apart from one scare, they didn't really threaten. We didn't look like a side which will be at the wrong end of the table on the showing today. Promising.

Hagrid: *we've won 2 games this season and Vernon's played in both. I said last season he was under-appreciated and I think he does a lot of work unnoticed. I think he is a very intelligent footballer and we look a better side with him in the team. But it's all about opinions, isn't it?*

WEEK 18

Frustration continued over where the money had gone and the strategy of manager Russell Slade following a 4-1 drubbing at Mansfield, which banished any memories of the apparent progress against Crewe.

Balthazar Bullitt *An afternoon of utter gash. They had tactics and we didn't. They had a semblance of a team and we had 11 blokes who all wear the same shirt.*

After last week I allowed myself to think that we were starting to "form" ourselves into something greater than the whole. This week was just a collection of holes.

Dixon and Mills were given the runaround and constantly being pulled out of position. Dixon, in particular, looks very vulnerable.

Hooper (who I actually thought was doing ok in the games I've seen him) just thought he had done enough by getting on the coach. He didn't even look arsed in the warm-up.

Rose (another I thought showed promise) was as invisible as two invisible James Berret's today. How he had the nerve to try and persuade Jones he should take the pen is beyond me!

Berrett (who I don't think is much cop) tried his best and at least made some passes to his colleagues.

Vernon. Stupid decisions from someone who I thought was an intelligent player (if you give him the ball below his chin). The one decent cross we put it all afternoon, just crying out for him to head back across the keeper and he tries to bring it down and loses it. A clear chance of a shot from 10 yards out and he passes it and we lose it.

Giving away needless free kicks around the box. Unable to defend set pieces. Zero fucking leadership evident from anyone, on or off the pitch. Nothing that looks like team spirit.

There is such a lack of discipline in that squad I do wonder what Slades does with them all week. Yes, Fenty is responsible for hiring him and for the budget, but shite on a bike you'd think there would be some semblance of teamwork.

It is utterly irrelevant whether you've managed and/or played five gadzillion games at a higher level. You ain't at that fucking level now and what you've done before means sod all

The Old Codger: *At least Bignot seemed to have a plan. Slade seems to prefer quantity over quality. It's just my opinion, but Bignot seemed to have a bigger plan than Fenty was prepared to finance and we're now left with a manager on the way down rather than one on the way up.*

davmariner: *Special mention to Nathan Clarke for how shite he's been since he arrived. I can't believe Slade got rid of Shaun Pearson for that donkey.*

RoboCod: *Just one thing I want to hear for Mr Fenty: that Slade has two months to turn this around, and get us looking like a top 10 team at the very least or he is GONE. If it's a good enough rule for Bignot, it's good enough for Slade.*

WEEK 19

Town's topsy-turvy season continued with a 2-1 midweek win at Accrington.

Horsforthmariner: *I'm absolutely freezing and still pretty wet! It was a good result and a decent performance.*

In the first half we started brightly before Accrington came into the game. Jones's goal came against the run of the play. We then got sucker punched with some poor defending.

In the second half we were the better side and Wolford's goal was very well taken.

Overall Matt was my MOTM, an absolute nightmare for defenders, he won plenty of headers, used his physical presence really well and looks the part. He worked his backside off too. I think he is the best striker we have.

Jones and Dembele both did really well and Woolford looks like he's got a lot of technical ability and he caused their full back loads of problems.

On the negative side - all our defenders were over 30 and it showed, Clarke and Collins didn't convince me.

I think we've got enough quality to not be in the relegation scrap but nowhere near enough for a top 7 finish.

TO HELL AND BACK

Meanwhile, Shrewsbury with ex-Town boss Paul Hurst and several ex-GTFC players were making a great start in League One, much to the delight of Shrews fans.

---

trueblue89: Hi all, after reading your board a few times and seeing mixed reviews about our current gaffer Paul Hurst. As clearly visible, we are sitting top of the table but its very early days.

Since taking over from a fading out manager in Mickey Mellon we turned to Hurst to save the ship. Mission accomplished perfectly. Changing the whole mentality of the team. We went from "League One Ready" players who quite frankly looked like they were only with us to pick up an easy wage and go home to a hungry determined and close-knitted group of players who look so much fitter and more organised than our opposition. Long may it continue.

And you know we have got a few ex-GTFC players who in fact have been great.

Dean Henderson (loan) has quickly become a fans' favourite showing great maturity for such a youthful 'keeper. His passion doesn't go unnoticed when we score/win he celebrates with the supporters. He makes strings of top acrobatic saves and also has a safe pair of hands. He is destined for a bright future in the game.

Aristote Nsiala (Toto) still has a lot to learn in my eyes and can be rash with challenges, but has been an absolute rock at the back. He is growing game by game and looks very good.

Jon Nolan - WHAT A PLAYER. Has been compared to ex-Shrews' player Ryan Woods (currently at Brentford) and the diminutive ginger engine shows a great vision for the game and has proven he can dictate the game on his own. The signing of the season so far.

Alex Rodman. When signed in January he was nowhere near fit. He chipped in with the odd assist. After having pre-season we have seen a totally different player. He is such a threat from out wide and adding goals to his game

Lennel John-Lewis (The Shop) has featured a lot from the bench at present and has been a fine squad addition. He is helping to seal games with fantastic hold-up play.

We currently are odds-on favourites to finish bottom. We have such a hard-working and determined bunch that on paper are not the most glamorous but its working.

The links don't end there. You currently have a few of our ex-players in your ranks and a few who have been fans favourites

Ben Davies was a fantastic ball playmaking midfielder who was excellent from set-pieces. Such a disappointment when he chose money and went to Notts County.

Sean McAllister, a tidy little ball player when with Shrewsbury, his spell was cut short due to constant injury problems.

Luke Summerfield, like his father Kevin, played for us. A very good hard-working player who just happened to be at the right place at the wrong time. He should have been given longer at Shrewsbury in my opinion.

Scott Vernon, an intelligent striker who probably didn't show Shrews fans his best and paid for it.

Akwasi Asante was a loan player and is quite frankly one of many loan strikers who fell off the radar with our supporters. He was involved in a poor team at the time but never really showed any promise.

Wishing you all the best for the season, I do look how you guys get on and how ex-players get on.

#SALOP

Town followed up the win at Accrington with a 2-1 win at Blundell Park over Yeovil. Things were looking up, and Grimsby had won 3 out of 4 and 2 out of 2 at Blundell Park.

---

headingly_mariner: Not pretty, but a well-deserved win. MOTM was a toss-up between Berrett and the impressive Woolford. If you're one of the few that booed Vernon on you're a total cunt.

Hagrid I would just also like to add the abuse Summerfield got from around me was completely out of order. If it was 1 bad pass in 10 it was straight on his back and "get him off he's fucking shit" all game long until the old man told them to get the eff off his back. I'm only 22 and I don't know if this a new thing, but there always seems to be a scapegoat at GTFC. It's a real downside of our fanbase.

WEEK 20

The pattern of last season was starting to develop. Just when Town managed a couple of wins, and optimism started to surface, along would come a defeat and it was back to square one. At Newport, County striker Padraig Amond came back like a bad penny to score the game's only goal. Ex-Mariner Amond had repeated the same feat last season when Grimsby had played Hartlepool, his club between Town and Newport.

__Grimal__ I've just got back from three enjoyable days staying with friends in Newport. I'm sorry to say the only disappointment was the first 45 minutes of the match, we could easily have been 4 -o down in the first 20 minutes if it wasn't for some excellent blocks from Macca and another headed off the line by I think it was Clark and have to say some pretty dire shooting from the Newport forwards. Rose was having a 'mare and wasn't surprised to see him replaced at halftime.

In the first half, we didn't look to have a clue how to clear our own box and the ball was continually coming straight back into the danger area; I thought here we go again another performance like Crewe away last season. God knows how we kept it to 0-0 at halftime. As the second half got underway I was pleased to see Summerfield who as of late has played well, on for Rose, I'm sure Slade must have stuck a rocket up their arses as they played like a completely different team. I never thought that Summerfield would ever transform a game but yesterday he for me was MOTM by a mile. We also looked much more of a threat when DJ replaced Dembele, both Summerfield and DJ deserve a start on Tuesday. The Amond goal was from a long throw into our box and the usual gift goal handed on a plate, once again terrible defensive marking, we know what Amond is, a jack in the box and he was completely unmarked. We huffed and puffed and on the second half display, in my opinion, we just shaded it and perhaps deserved something out the game. On Saturday morning I had a walk around Newport shopping precinct I bumped into a young man named Padraig Amond, he was with a middle-aged couple, perhaps his mother and father. I had a bit of a chat and said to him in a jovial way that he's going to be playing for the wrong team that afternoon and he replied to me in a quite serious way that "He didn't want me", I don't really know who he meant by "He". I replied to him, that everyone else would have been very happy for him to be playing for GTFC. I jokingly said "don't you score against us today" and he just replied "I'll try". I'm not sure if he meant try not to score or I'll try to score :). Anyway, he's a likeable young man. We move on and hopefully three points on Tuesday night. UTM.

Rob Sedgwick

GTFC Director John Fenty made one of his occasional forays onto the forum try and clear up the background to a some of the perennial issues that get raised about shares.

JF: *Good morning my Fishy Friends,*

It seems the flack continues towards me over the transfer of Trust shares to me, 200,000 of them.

I've asked the Trust in the past to clear such matters up as the flack isn't justified at all, but in the absence, I will.

It's very true that in the situation I found myself through no fault of mine, that control did not sit within the boardroom.

To my recollection, I don't recall ever stating that we would have to sell Liam Hearn, but it was the case that I stated I wouldn't put another penny in the club until shareholding control in the boardroom was restored.

It was a fact that by the December the Club needed funds without which speculation suggested we might need to sell a player. (Liam Hearn)

It is a fact that the Chair of the Trust and the CEO of the Club negotiated the proposal put to me.

At no time and to be very clear, did I coerce those discussions whatsoever, or was involved in meetings where they were discussed with members of the Trust.

Following Trust members voting for a Transfer to me of the said block of shares, I then proposed that I would purchase £200.000 additional shares - in effect balancing the proposal.

There were several other ways my concerns could have been met, with or without transferring of the shares, but this is what was put to me and I accepted in the best interests of the club.

I'm sure some will continue to twist these facts, but for the genuine fans that may want to know, this puts the record straight.

Kind regards John Fenty

UTM

That predictably would never silence the fiercest of the critics:

Marinerz93: *There seems to be spin or twisting as you seem to call it.*

Both you and Parker agreed to fund the club £500K after Parker stated that benign loans are bad for the books, and attracting new investors.

Why did you and the board allow Parker to buy £500K worth of shares and then not match it as you had already agreed to match Parker's investment? By allowing Parker to have more shares meant Article 9 came into force, are you telling us that you weren't aware of the rules regarding shareholding?

Parker showed his business skills when he gifted the trust £500k worth of shares because this meant he wasn't forced to buy your shares or have the club without its assets. Why did you put a covenant on the Trust not to accept any more shares from Mike Parker?

Please set the record straight because the shares fiasco will rumble on if you matched MP the trust would never have the shares and control would still have been in the boardroom. Genuine fans would like it as it was with no spin.

But there were good things said about JF as well.

Zmariner: *Watch the celebration at the end of the FGR win and see if Mr Fenty is a fan, I do not agree with all but for me, he is a Town fanatic absolutely no doubt at all*

Grimsby Pete: *I have not been told or asked to be quiet on here and I am free to say what I think is true,*

BUT

Having spoken to John on the phone I can see both sides and I understand certain things could be upsetting if the same thing was said to me.

So whatever anybody thinks of John I can say he is very approachable and is willing to talk to any fan.

Off the field life's events were happily progressing

Davmariner. *Given that the mood seems to have been a bit dark on here recently, it's worth mentioning one piece of good news that McKeown's fiance gave birth to a baby girl earlier on. Congrats to both of them and hope mum and baby are both doing well!*

The issue of prejudice (on the site's Player Ratings feature for each game) was raised. Ironically the poster sounds slightly prejudiced himself.

Maringer. *Dixon who played well, didn't put a foot wrong and was awarded man of the match, gets the lowest score there. It says all you need to know about how prejudiced against some players from the off some fans are.*

Summerfield played well, full stop. If he was capable of playing at that level all the time, I'd be happy enough to see him as a regular, but he's not.

WEEK 21

An inconsistent month had seen 3 wins and 2 losses. In the final week of September came two draws, both at Blundell Park. Firstly, came Colchester when a last-minute Sam Jones penalty rescued a point for Town. A 2-2 draw with a late equaliser sounds exciting but failed to inspire the fans

---

moosey_club: *well that was just...shit wasn't it? No dressing it up from anyone please.....it was just crap...*

3300 odd home supporters.....isn't that about the total of STH this year? down to the bare bones hardcore already...and I didn't hear a single happy voice all the way home.

Uninspiring garbage.

The news that Chris Clements (who had been one of the better midfielders the year before but been sent on loan by Slade and never used by Town all season) was free to leave was greeted with disappointment

---

Mariner_09: *I don't know why anyone's surprised. He's a midfielder who can play football and Slade doesn't like those.*

Jonnyboy82: *Clements while not himself the best midfielder in league 2 by a long shot he is better than Summerfield and Berrett. It's times like this when I think why just why.*

scott_gtfc_89: *I'd rather have Clements any day of the week than Summerfield or Berrett. A great signing for them will score a few in that league as well. A shocking decision, just like the Pearson one, over what we have signed*

Slade out.

The Lincoln derby at least offered the prospect of some excitement in a one-off derby game.

Maringer: *If you don't want to watch your team play a local derby against your oldest rivals in a game where a win will potentially take you above them in the table when exactly do you want to watch them?*

With our indifferent form at present, I can understand why some might not want to go to a Tuesday night match against Colchester, but surely the whole point about following a team is wanting to get one over your local rivals in the 'big' games? ;)

But it failed to provide any as it ended in an utterly dull 0-0 draw in front of over 7,500 fans

---

ginnywings *As derbies go that was fairly tame and not much to get excited about. The much-vaunted Lincoln looked no better than us apart from Raggett, who is clearly a level above. A draw was a fair result and once the excellent Summerfield went off, it was obvious that Slade was just bothered about keeping things tight. I thought Matt was terrible and Dixon had a bit of a stinker again, but all the others did their job. No side looked good enough to take the game by the scruff of the neck and get a winner.*

Overall, the game was drab and lacking entertainment.

Only Summerfield was drawing any plaudits at this stage of the season, but only from some sections of the crowd.

---

mimma *Why can't you leave Summerfield alone? He was head and shoulders above every other player on the pitch. What has he got to do for you to acknowledge he's done well?*

Even when he has a really good game you still knock him.

It must be a Grimsby thing. Once a player is deemed not good enough then they are automatically labelled rubbish no matter how well they played.

Grimsby had pulled clear of the bottom two and had returned to their customary "spot" betwixt and between the promotion scene and the danger zone.

Pos	Team	P	W	D	L	F	A	GD	Pts
1	Notts County	11	8	1	2	21	11	+10	25
2	Exeter	11	8	1	2	20	12	+8	25
3	Accrington	11	7	2	2	21	13	+8	23
4	Coventry	11	7	1	3	14	6	+8	22
5	Luton	11	6	3	2	21	10	+11	21
6	Stevenage	11	6	3	2	19	12	+7	21
7	Wycombe	11	6	3	2	22	17	+5	21
8	Mansfield	11	5	4	2	18	13	+5	19
9	Swindon	11	6	1	4	16	14	+2	19
10	Newport County	11	5	3	3	15	12	+3	18
11	Lincoln	11	4	4	3	13	12	+1	16
12	Cambridge	11	5	1	5	11	11	0	16
13	Cheltenham	11	4	2	5	14	13	+1	14
14	Carlisle	11	4	2	5	15	16	-1	14
15	Grimsby	11	4	2	5	14	18	-4	14
16	Colchester	11	3	3	5	16	18	-2	12
17	Yeovil	11	3	3	5	17	24	-7	12
18	Barnet	11	3	2	6	15	16	-1	11
19	Crewe	11	3	2	6	12	18	-6	11
20	Crawley Town	11	3	1	7	11	14	-3	10
21	Morecambe	11	2	4	5	10	16	-6	10
22	Port Vale	11	1	2	8	8	17	-9	5
23	Chesterfield	11	1	2	8	9	23	-14	5
24	Forest Green	11	1	2	8	10	26	-16	5

League Table 30th September

OCTOBER

Grimsby Nil

WEEK 22

Town continued their miserable record in the Checkatrade with a 2-1 defeat at Scunthorpe watched by less than 250 people.

RichMariner: *What a thoroughly boring competition this is.*

Our reserve team playing Scunny's reserve team, and the glory of our reserve team playing Sunderland's B team to come.

Good work, Harvey. Good work. Give yourself a bonus and an extra pat on the back for ruining the thing you're paid handsomely to improve.

Meanwhile, Town's impressive away form continued with a 2-1 win over Port Vale. The boring style of football was grinding out the results but led to the existential question of whether we watch to be entertained or to win.

Hagrid: *A game of two halves like I've never known. The first half was dreadful, a lot of anger and murmurings on the terraces, we created nothing and long ball football. In the second half the goal changed everything, we passed our way through Port Vale, attacked on the wings and used Vernon's strengths especially. It was a fantastic build-up for the second goal with Dembele finishing superbly after an outstanding ball from Summerfield. Matt and Woolford had chances to extend the lead. We then sat back for the last 10 and put ourselves under pressure with balls into our box causing some concern. I thought Vale were poor but take nothing away from us, it* was an outstanding performance in the second half. Now we MUST back it up, and get some momentum going.

forza ivano (replying to a post demanding Slade be sacked): Christ on a bike, Slade out? I'm surprised Fenty, Slade et. al. don't walk away from the club when they read moronic comments like that. Just to remind you: Last 6 games: wins 3, drawn 2, lost 1. That's 11 points in 6 games, which over the season would result in c. 85 points. Still, I suppose even quoting facts like that is pointless with brain dead idiots like you.

Theimperialcoroner: I personally think his footy style is more turgid than a night out in Goole, but a win is a win is a win.

WEEK 23

Town had yet another 0-0 home draw with Crawley and the debate around "entertainment" dominated. Grimsby should have won but Jones missed an opportunity for three points when he struck a late penalty wide.

ginnywings: Wow! That was fucking awful. A game so drab that the only thing that could put the slightest gloss on it, is if we had managed to snatch the three points, but we fucked that up as well. To be fair to Jones, he won the penalty and was the only player from either side to look like troubling the defence. But we can't have any of that so Slade in his wisdom takes him off and brings on Hooper, a player so anonymous that I forgot he was on the pitch until he mis-controlled the ball in injury time.

I used to love football but it is getting increasingly harder and harder to enjoy. There is no guile, no craft, no crosses, no shots, no goalmouth scrambles, just two sides of extremely fit and organised players taking it in turns to hoof the ball from one end of the pitch to the other, with the odd attempt to try a bit of football, which usually lasts about three passes before possession is given away. I totally regret buying a season ticket now because the stuff on offer is garbage and the crowd is dead.

Oh, and the ref was shite. Blowing his whistle every 20 seconds it felt like.

The endless debate over style versus results continued with some fellow Grimsby supporters even coming to blows on the way home.

Croxton: *I wanted to wait for a more positive theme for my first post but needs must! Whilst trudging back to my car along Grimsby Road near Tesco Express, I foolishly butted in on a conversation between two fans I took to be a father and son (in his Twenties?). They were clearly upset by the booing and repeated 'negativity' of the home crowd. I said that fans have paid their money and will vent their feelings. They bemoaned the 'constant' demands of Grimsby fans for sacking managers and seemed to think I was suspect in this regard despite my making no references to Russell Slade. The younger man then verbally abused me. I told him that his manner was not necessary and was then pushed to the ground by a third man in his twenties who must have been behind me. I stood up and berated him for assaulting a pensioner. He said if I did not shut up, he would knock me out. As I write this, even I think it sounds as if I must have given them some cause to be enraged, but not so.*

I looked around for a police officer. Invisible. I witnessed the OTT police presence at Mansfield and Port Vale. Such a contrast!

This group of four or five 'adults' got into a car at the top of Phelps Street and left quickly. Yes, I failed to assess who I was talking to and should have made neutral responses and, having been decked, spared them the lecture. I will soon be 68 and Boylenesque in stature and have had many affable conversations with fellow Town fans home and away. I abhor victimhood and hold myself partially responsible for this undignified affair but I just felt that the matter should be aired so others may be more guarded than myself.

As I drove the seventy miles home I listened to Russell's interview and sighed. Chaos33 got it right today.

BackHeelTony: *I really don't understand why so many people are so concerned about the style of play.*

I have no doubt that in time Slade will give us winning football. We will improve and be fighting for promotion before too long. Do we really have to play like Brazil to get there?

Let's have some patience, get behind the team and let the manager do things his way.

ginnywings *(in reply): Because football isn't just about results. Had the pen gone in and we had won, it still would have been boring beyond belief.*

Heppy88: *Watching football this season at Blundell Park is soul destroying. There is not one ounce of entertainment on offer. I have never been so disinterested, dispassionate and outright bored at a football match.*

Having a season ticket feels like a ball and chain this season. The problem is it's hard to see where any improvement will come from. Sladeball = Shiteball. Slade Out!

With Osborne/Asante still absent on loan, some fans were questioning whether they would be better in the team, but the official explanation of an opportunity for players to regain fitness won some support.

---

ginnywings: *A month of competitive games with Solihull will get him match fit and sharp quicker than the odd reserve game and fleeting sub appearances surely? Same with Clements at Barrow.*

Am I the only one who thinks this is a good thing?

WEEK 24

There were two ways of looking at recent results. The "half empty" posters looked at the negatives and the "half full" brigade looked at the positives. It felt like Grimsby were not playing well but they were grinding out enough results to maintain a respectable position in the table.

Jarmo.Is.God: *1 loss in 7 and 2 home clean sheets in a row. Or 1 win in 5, and not scored in 2 home games*

13 games in and only Jones has scored more than 2...

After 13 games, we have 18 points, and we are only 5 points off the play-offs and 12 points above the relegation zone

This time last season we only had 2 more points under Hurst who everyone seems to love and wish we never let go. Yet Slade needs to go?

After 13 games last season, Blackpool had 14 points, and Exeter had 13 points... these met in the play-off final.

There is more to it than the above, I get that, as Saturday was one of the worst games I've been to in a long long time.

However, if you didn't know the table, or results, and read this forum, you would think we were in Chesterfield's place right now...

The visiting faithful were treated to a 3-2 thriller at Cheltenham, belying the dull fare at Blundell Park.

Barralad *Well that was a nervy last 10!! The first half was exceptional. They couldn't handle Dembele at all. Some of his footwork is simply outrageous. On one occasion he took a high ball down flicked it up and round the defender. It was worth the cost of the day on his own. But It was far from a one-man show. Summerfield was magnificent. Just about everything we did involved him. Woolford's ball to Siriki for the first goal was perfect. Both centre backs were immense against Cheltenham's high ball game with the only blot being Pell's free header for their goal. In the second half, it was clear Dembele was struggling a bit well before he came off. I don't know if Son of madeley was at the game but Town dealt pretty comfortably with anything the home team slung in until that last 10. Their second goal was decent and our old giving free-kicks away in dangerous areas resurfaced but somehow (with a bit of help from their crap finishing) we held on. The much-maligned Dixon made some crucial first-half tackles and blocks. Summerfield my MOTM just edged Dembele but what a talent he is!*

The Mariners continued their fine away form with a 0-0 draw at Morecambe. As ever, some were happier than others with a point. The goal drought continued nonetheless.

Hagrid In the Conference days it's a game we would have lost. It's a point gained, well done team

Skrill Shout out to the absolutely amazing 462 Mariners who went all the way to Morecambe!

GyMariner draws get you nowhere in football due to the points system.
It's all well and good not losing but when you think 2 losses and 1 win is equivalent to 3 draws it's not that pretty.

oldun (in reply): Yes but we have picked up 4 points this week from 2 away games. Promotion form. We need to back it up with a long overdue home win on Sat.

WEEK 25

The Football League report concluded that no action should be taken against Stevenage for "Bragate".

Bigdog EFL STATEMENT: STEVENAGE V GRIMSBY TOWN

Following a comprehensive review of events alleged to have taken place prior to the League Two fixture between Stevenage and Grimsby Town on Saturday 19th August, the EFL has now given due consideration to the complaint raised in respect of the stewarding operation on the day
.
On receipt of detailed observations from both Clubs, the EFL can confirm that no specific action is to be taken under its rules.

The EFL will, however, continue to work with all its Clubs to ensure that attending matches remains an enjoyable, positive experience for supporters and to assist will be issuing updated guidance regarding a number of safety, security and stewarding matters. In addition, supporters are reminded that dedicated channels exist at all Clubs and the EFL to ensure that there are professional and approachable points of contact to report any complaints or issues of concern.

Details are available via a Club's or the EFL's Supporters' Charter.

Alternatively, all supporters have the right to contact the Independent Football Ombudsman (IFO) who are accredited as an Approved Alternate Dispute Resolution Body.

The EFL notes the cooperation received in this matter and in particular would like to thank both the management teams at Stevenage and Grimsby Town for their assistance.

-
ENDS

The EFL are spineless and not fit for purpose.

The club at Grimsby refused though to back the fans' demands for action, despite requests from the Trust board. Were the two clubs closing ranks?

Bax: *For the record, speaking as the Vice Chair of the Trust, I really do hope the club comes out and supports the fans on this. And I think for every minute that ticks by with silence, they are making a huge mistake.*

Realist: *Fenty is part of the EFL machine. That is why he voted against the fans' wishes on the EFL Trophy. He is spineless and only appears interested in bullying fans who speak against him on this forum. How about speaking up FOR your fans for once?*

Reverendmariner: *I feel very strongly that this matter should not be allowed to drift away. It's appalling that the EFL should decide that no action should be taken because an alleged safeguarding offence has taken place. I don't believe that it is up to Mr Fenty to issue a statement; the club's admirable Customer Charter of 2017, which is available on the internet, identifies Martin George as the club's Safeguarding Officer. Surely it is up to Mr George to try to contact the alleged victims, which would not be difficult through this forum, gather information, and if the alleged victims were willing to make an official complaint, to submit a report to Hertfordshire Police. Safeguarding is not merely concerned with the care of children and vulnerable adults. It would then have to be investigated; the Police would have no choice. It is a legal matter rather than a question of PR. In many other fields, such investigations, both of recent and historic allegations, have been and remain exhaustive, and this case should be no different.*

Meanwhile the much-vaunted away points were not followed by a home performance to back it up, and yet another 0-0 draw, this time against Cambridge, was played out.

Arryarryarry. *Slade deserved to be booed. Taking off your top scorer and the only player who looked like scoring for in my opinion the laziest no.9 [Hooper] I have seen in over 50 years and leaving Vernon on who wouldn't have scored if he was still on the pitch on his own. No wonder Jones looked pissed off.*

Also taking off Town's most exciting player who had 2 shots at goal and one great run to the byline before putting in a very good cross while leaving on Woolford who did frig all. No wonder the fans chanted "you don't know what you're doing"

The lack of entertainment was the final straw for many fans who were regretting buying season tickets.

TheCodfather1966. *How people can go and watch Town for 40-odd years, and then suddenly lose all interest........... but slowly maybe I can see how this can happen. I accept that our league position is reasonable in a crap division, but this season's home performances have killed my interest in watching Town this season. Our football is dreadful, we seem clueless week in week out and the entertainment value is 1/10 nearly every home game. How and when did we become so negative??? When the opposition have a corner, why do we never leave a player upfield so the ball doesn't ping straight back in our goalmouth?!!! Why do we constantly take off our potentially match-winning players? Thank frig the next two games are away from home. I will never stop going to see Town after this length of time, but bloody hell, give us something to get excited about once in a while. I am starting to think Slade was a poor appointment for us, even though our league position is acceptable. I will give Slade credit for something though. It must be a first at Blundell Park that our league position is reasonable, but the team and management still get booed off on a regular basis.......*

The league table at the end of October was looking a lot healthier. Town fans were definitely looking upward at this stage, with the Mariners just four points off the play-offs and heading northwards. The football might have been boring, but success ultimately came down to what position Town occupied in the table.

Pos	Team	P	W	D	L	F	A	GD	Pts
1	Notts County	16	10	3	3	28	16	+12	33
2	Accrington	16	10	2	4	30	19	+11	32
3	Luton	16	9	4	3	34	15	+19	31
4	Exeter	16	9	3	4	23	18	+5	30
5	Swindon	16	9	1	6	24	18	+6	28
6	Coventry	16	8	3	5	17	8	+9	27
7	Wycombe	16	7	6	3	31	25	+6	27
8	Newport County	16	7	4	5	23	18	+5	25
9	Lincoln	16	6	6	4	16	14	+2	24
10	Cambridge	16	7	3	6	16	16	0	24
11	Stevenage	16	7	3	6	24	27	-3	24
12	Grimsby	16	6	5	5	19	21	-2	23
13	Colchester	16	6	4	6	23	21	+2	22
14	Mansfield	16	5	7	4	22	21	+1	22
15	Cheltenham	16	6	3	7	23	23	0	21
16	Carlisle	16	5	5	6	22	23	-1	20
17	Yeovil	16	5	4	7	24	29	-5	19
18	Crewe	16	5	2	9	16	25	-9	17
19	Crawley Town	16	4	4	8	12	16	-4	16
20	Forest Green	16	4	3	9	16	32	-16	15
21	Barnet	16	3	5	8	19	24	-5	14
22	Port Vale	16	4	2	10	16	23	-7	14
23	Morecambe	16	3	5	8	12	22	-10	14
24	Chesterfield	16	2	3	11	15	31	-16	9

League Table 31st October

NOVEMBER

Treading Water

WEEK 26

The SLO was nominated for an award following her excellent work in the coverage after Bragate at Stevenage:http://www.fsf.org.uk/latest-news/view/fsf-awards-2017-shortlists-announced

---

PoshHarry: *Kristine has been nominated for an award for her work as the Supporter Liaison Officer by The Football Supporters Federation.*

It does not look like it is a public vote unfortunately but good luck Kristine, it is great to see that your hard work is being recognised in the industry and well as many of the Fishy people who really appreciate the help, information and advice you provide on here.

The club accounts were issued which showed that Grimsby Town FC had made over £800K from player trading in the last year and a loan had been paid back to John Fenty, which turned out to be a short-term loan from him to finance the play-off match at Wembley when Town got promoted.

Statement:https://www.grimsby-townfc.co.uk/news/2017/november/club-statement---2017-accounts/

---

forza ivano: *All in all an excellent set of accounts, with the result that we are on a far more even keel than we have been for years. The other nice thing is that 3 factors could still be* *advantageous to us. a) if we could get any sort of FA cup run, b) if Dembele was to go, as rumoured, in January and c) if Osborne or A.N.Other comes through and we are able to sell them on. It would be lovely to get to a position in 12 months time where JF is more or less paid off and we are basically spending what we bring in.*

GrimRob: *I wonder what it has actually cost us to appoint and sack two managers and two assistants? Plus pay quite a few players who have hardly kicked a ball. If we had a smaller, more settled squad it seems to me we could afford to splash out on a couple of top quality players. Our wage bill has been bloated for too long with quantity rather than quality.*

Town were dumped out of the FA Cup 1-0 by Plymouth, another cup defeat to continue the 100% record of cup losses that had taken place since Town's promotion to the Football League.

---

penrith mariner: *I don't post very often and don't like to criticise, but here goes. Yet another game this season where I've left after 90 minutes feeling so frustrated. Why Do we have to be so negative? Today was not a bad performance, not great, but in brief spells, we showed what we could be capable of.*

I thought we looked good for the first 10 minutes without really threatening their goal. We conceded a soft goal with Plymouth's second venture into our half. Carey glided past 3 of our defenders without a proper challenge then curled a great shot into the top corner. Plymouth are a poor side, without Carey they would be a lot worse. Similar could be said of ourselves with Dembele!

Carey continued to cause chaos in the Town defence throughout the first half, running rings round Dixon. A good save from Macca from a Carey free-kick kept Town in the game but basically that summed up a poor first half.

The second half started the same as the first half ended. WHY NO SUBS???

To be honest for the first 20 minutes of the 2nd half I was bored. The midfield was too deep, the front two put lots of effort in but there was no end result. The defence coped better with Carey. The game was lit up by two pieces of pure brilliance from Dembele, the first beating two players on the edge of the box before hitting a great left foot shot to the top left corner. A great save by the Argyle keeper. The second was one of the finest pieces of football I have seen in years, receiving the ball in midfield he had 5 players around him, a turn, two drag backs another turn and a nutmeg and he had beaten all 5 of them. This guy is really special.

Last 20 minutes and at last the subs we have been craving for came on, DJ on for Woolford and Matt on for an ineffective Vernon. Unfortunately for the next 10 minutes, we couldn't get a foothold in the game. Dembele seemed to be suffering from cramp and was replaced by Cardwell. The last 10 minutes of the game was by far our best spell of the game. Throwing everything at them creating numerous chances but just not getting the final touch.

Personally I thought the score was a fair reflection of the game.

The questions that I want to be answered:
Why do we continue to be so negative? When we attack we look good.
Why can we not start a game with Dembele and DJ?
What does Cardwell need to to to be given a fair chance?
The big question.....when I pay to go to a football match, should I EXPECT to be entertained??

The Old Codger "Grimsby Nil" for the 6th time in the last 10 games - getting a bit of a problem Mr Slade.

WEEK 27

Just 248 turned up to watch Sunderland U-23 in the Checkatrade Trophy which prompted GTFC Accounts Manager Steve Wraith to accuse Town fans who wanted to boycott the tournament of bullying supporters into not attending the game.

Link:http://www.grimsbytelegraph.co.uk/sport/football/grimsby-town-fans-should-not-749750

MarinersOnTheUp The article on the Telegraph website is an absolute insult. Unbelievable. Who exactly do some people at the club think they are?

I'm sorry but nobody has been bullied into not attending. We stayed away because we refuse to support something that could lead to more damage than good.

Who the hell do people at the club think they are to accuse us of bullying other fans into staying away? Why should we back the Checkatrade trophy and the corrupt, incompetent EFL when we've made our feelings clear that we don't want B teams? I'm particularly angry that the club come out with that rubbish, yet it was the club (John Fenty and the board) that voted in favour of B-teams despite knowing fans didn't want it. How can fans be accused of bullying other fans into staying away when the club themselves knowingly voted against the fans' wishes. Did nobody consider that people stayed away because:

a) Fans don't like the format of the competition

b) We don't want B-teams invading our competitions, potentially leading to their introduction to the league system.

c) We don't want to support more nonsense from the EFL

d) There was nothing to play for anyway

e) The football on show is dire

f) As I already mentioned, the club voted in favour of B teams despite knowing GTFC fans didn't agree with it.

I'm totally fed up of being treated so poorly as a fan by the club I love. Changes are needed higher up, ASAP.

I am so disappointed.

The divide between the fans and the club is wider than the Humber at the minute.

No one at the club has any idea what the fans want. That's because they don't listen to us and, crucially, they don't want to listen to us.

If Steve Wraith had made any attempt to reach out to the fans, read this message board or physically talked to fans on a match day about their feelings towards the trophy competition, he'd have known that none of us had bullied anyone into not going.

But no. He's just thrown an attitude at the whole subject without making the tiniest effort to engage with us.

His attitude is reflective of the club. No effort, no time, no desire to do what's best.

Do as we say, not do as we do.

They just expect us to turn up every week and hand over our hard-earned money, no questions asked.

If GTFC was a traditional business, it would've folded years ago. They leech off our loyalty. They've always relied on our loyalty. And last night was the first time in our ENTIRE HISTORY that our loyal troops seriously turned their back on the club and they hit a massive red panic button.

Last night was entirely the result of THEIR doing, not ours.

I really hope last night marked a turning point - the moment when the club finally listened and acted on it.

They have a chance to do that, but I'm not holding my breath.

After the break for cups Town lost the first two league games of November. For the first time, the "Slade Out" posts were starting to get lots of green ticks.

Jonnyboy82: The sooner our non-chairman sacks this dinosaur and looks at what he really wants for this club the better.

We make Hurst look like Guardiola at the minute and I ain't paying 18 quid anymore to get neck ache.

I'm fuming as we are going nowhere fast.

TheCodfather1966: Yet another nil. This clown must surely get sacked now, he has been nothing short of abysmal. I don't even think I can be bothered to go next Saturday to watch us record another nil and probably lose. I wish another Chairman with a few quid would step in to replace Fenty as well. He has been the curse of GTFC over the past decade.

Make some changes, Board of Directors, whilst we still have 3,000 fans left FFS....................

Bigdog: Anyone else get the feeling that we're not safe from the drop this season?

Mendonca1995: Having to watch him play Vernon up front and Woolford left wing every week breaks my heart compared to what we have had. We can't score goals and half the squad that we have got aren't good enough and are on big 2-year final paydays!!! IT'S BORING TO WATCH AND NOT GOOD ENOUGH

Jarmo.Is.God: I've watched Town for just under 20 years. My dad used to take me, then I took my younger brother.

I've got the badge as a tattoo on me, basically, I'm a massive and passionate fan. Yet I've never felt so disinterested about them in all my time. I didn't even know our line-up yesterday until half 3 when I was told...

I use to go out my way to make sure I was at every home game, and as many away games as possible, and I now don't even bother going to most home games.

I have a 20-month-old son, and would rather sit at home with him, then pay money to get frustrated and angry.

And there is no chance of taking him to Blundell Park any day soon, the last thing I want is the NSPCC knocking on my door...

With the incessant problem of nobody but John Fenty willing and able to run the club, some started to consider fan ownership

---

jock dock tower: I have consistently argued on here about the benefits of fans owning football clubs. There have been some in support of it, but mainly it's about "we can't service the loans etc"

I sense the tide is slowly but surely turning towards fans possibly now being in favour of such a move? The pronouncements from BP about bullying, their backing of the Checkatrade Trophy, little comment on Bragate and numerous other PR gaffes highlight the problems of the kind of control any individual can hold over a club when the views of the fans are not taken into account. I think it's fair to say had the Trust been running the club on behalf of the fans then at the very least, there would have been some kind of consultation on such issues. True, some of the things wouldn't have changed, we'd still be playing in the Checkatrade Trophy, and the EFL would probably have ignored pleas made by the Trust in terms of Bragate, but at least the fans would be comforted by the fact that THEIR club was speaking out on THEIR behalf.

Fan ownership has to come sometime. If it's good enough for La Liga and the Bundesliga, its time has surely come for Town?

WEEK 28

Another home-defeat, 1-0 to Carlisle, predictably stirred the hornets' nest, and Town once again failed to score at home.

---

ginnywings: *Not much to report really. It was much better than the last home game and we were better than Carlisle, who looked just as poor as every other side that have come here this season, but as is our wont, we gifted them a goal with poor marking and you just knew we wouldn't get a serious shot at their goal after that, never mind an equaliser. We rotated the front players today and none of them looks like a proper striker.*

Two poor sides, boring as fuck. Apathy reigns at BP.

Mimma: *Not leaving a player up when defending a corner is criminal. Even more so when a goal down.*

The football is awful under Slade. Too negative, frightened to attack, stand off, always second to the ball, no belief.

When they had the ball they had options, with players moving into space to receive the ball. We were the exact opposite. When we have the ball there is no movement whatsoever resulting in aimless balls that are easy to defend. We are too quick to get back to defend but very slow to attack when we get it.

Something has to give soon, and it will be Slade that goes, paying the price on percentage football with no skill involved.

Middle-aged Town fans who remembered the years in the Championship during the 1980s and 1990s were finding it hard to come to terms with life in the lower echelons of the professional game.

Gainsbro_Mariner: *I've been a Grimsby Town supporter for all my life, I've been a poster on the Fishy since the days of the original Electronic Fishcake rivals.net days (1999 I believe). I've seen this club have great days and some damned right horrible days. This is my first proper post in a long time, but I feel like many of you I need to get this off my chest.*

Rob Sedgwick

Although I live in exile (a lot further than Gainsborough these days) I still invest a lot of my time into supporting Town although I don't get back home as much these days. There is no way we can sugar coat or beat around the bush any longer, change at the top is needed and with all due respect to Mr Fenty I just feel this club cannot get to where it aspires to be whilst the current leadership is in place. Those of us who are old enough to remember us playing in the Championship on a regular basis expect us to be aspiring to be that club once more. Before you had the saying "but can you do it on a wet Tuesday night in Stoke" it was "can you do it on a wet Tuesday night on Blundell Park", this club may have always been a relegation struggler in those days but we gave as good as we got and we wouldn't care if you're Sunderland, Forest, Wednesday or Manchester City we were capable of winning and you'd have to be at your best to play us off our own ground.

The biggest issue for this club's decline is the new stadium issue! I was at secondary school when we announced that we were building the Conoco Stadium and here I am now in my 30's and we are no closer to building it, in fact, we even further away. It's sickening for me to name clubs who were in a worse position, lower division and in some cases a worse financial state who have built stadiums since we made our initial announcement. - Hull City. Doncaster Rovers, Swansea City, Cardiff City, Colchester United, Chesterfield, Rotherham United and be assured to add Scunthorpe United and maybe Lincoln City to that list in the future. I'm sure the blame doesn't lay solely at the feet of the board but you've got to wonder why it's so hard for us to grow us a club? Especially in earlier years.

I'm going to fast-forward to the summer of 2016, we'd been promoted with a fantastic set of players put together by a manager who was often criticised for not getting us back in the Football League sooner. Our fans were famed nationwide for being loyal, passionate and attending away games in their droves. A lot of people including me actually thought we were capable of back to back promotions. Hurst leaves and Bignot arrives and the board invest money and faith into this up and coming young manager. A few months later he's abruptly dismissed because we sit in mid-table with Fenty citing that we had an alarmingly large squad of players amongst other reasons. It appears to me that the board just fed Bignot rope to hang himself from Day 1! Who sanctioned these transfers? If this was a big issue why was he not told to calm it?

So then Russell Slade is lined up to return, a guy who despite taking us to the 2006 Play-Off Final and beating Spurs in the League Cup was largely unpopular for numerous reasons, one of which being his negative unattractive and sometimes ineffective brand of football. I for one was in the minority and welcomed the return of RS despite said issues, seeing as he had gone on to manage in the Championship and League One since leaving us and having only managed Cardiff very recently then he may come back with a few new tricks and a phone book full of new contacts! Nevertheless, the football has been worse!

Over the summer I appreciate and understand not every player we look at and attempt to sign ends up coming, the rumblings of Nicky Maynard etc is all great until he chooses to his football elsewhere, so I can appreciate the frustration of the management team when our main targets go to another club. That being said our recruitment over the summer was negative. Not only did we allow guys like Shaun Pearson and Disley to move on, we chucked contracts at players such as Kelly and JJ Hooper who both looked iffy on and off paper. This kind of recruitment is what got us relegated in the first place. The club has spent so much money paying the wages of the Matthew Heywood's, Adrian Forbes, Serge Makofo's and Nick Colgan's of the world. Hurst had the transfer acumen to go down to buy non-league players of good standards and that's where your Liam Hearn's, Omar Bogle's and Shaun Pearson's came from! Slade may not have the knowledge of the part-time game but send your scouts out! Go and watch games! Why are we wasting money on signing players who look as bad as they are on paper and who haven't looked remotely sharp even on trial? He did it before with the likes of Clint Marcelle, Terry Barwick, Jermaine Palmer, Tommy Taylor, Glen Downey and Colin Cramb. All given contacts, all were not up to it and soon left.

The club is starting to alienate itself from the fans, the way this Curtis Woodhouse thing was dealt with was embarrassing. Some clubs even release a News section called "In the Papers" with all the latest gossip. Are Manchester United going to release several statements publicly slating a journalist because he speculated a former player may be joining the coaching staff? Is Fenty happy with the atmosphere? Is he happy with the falling crowds? Is he happy that the fans feel disconnected? But more importantly is he happy with the football that's on offer? As a fan base do we expect too much? I don't think we do. We expect to be challenging, we expect ambition, pride but mainly just common sense! Something that seems to be lacking in this club these days.

From nowhere a problem came after *Radio Humberside* reporter Matt Dean wrote a speculative tweet about Curtis Woodhouse. It was to explode into a major row between the club, the media and the fans. The tweet was initially dismissed, the anger showing in the wording.

Link:https://www.grimsby-townfc.co.uk/news/2017/november/curtis-woodhouse--more-inaccurate-reporting/

Bigdog: *Official GTFC Statement:-*

Grimsby Town Football Club wishes to end any speculation regarding the appointment of Curtis Woodhouse reported by a local media outlet.

At the request of Curtis, he was welcomed to Cheapside to witness a First Team training session to gain an insight and experience to help progress his own career and will not be joining the club.

That above is what the statement should have said. *No finger pointing, no public dressing down and it would have actually gained a bit of goodwill in the bank from RH and Matt Dean rather than make it so vitriolic.*

But no, there's a member of staff at GTFC that's finally rammed home an open goal. Where's the common decency? Reporter speculates about player, coach or manager at a football club. Big shock. We all want the transfer speculation off him in the transfer window, don't we?

No finesse, no thinking, no class in that statement. That sums up the PR standard at the club for me.

On top of that, Matt is a mild-mannered diehard Town fan and a thoroughly good bloke.

Chrisblor: *John Fenty is a pathetic baby. He can't wait to fire out a statement having a pop at Radio Humberside (who provide a much better standard of coverage for the club than the Telegraph by about a million miles), yet is still weirdly silent on issues like the EFL Stevenage whitewash and fan criticism of the Checkatrade Trophy. The sooner this tone-deaf squatter and his ancient benign loans are pried away from the club, the better.*

WEEK 29

Such is the uncertainty of football that Town shocked the fans with two wins in a week. The season certainly looked it was finally heading in a positive direction.

Firstly, Town beat Swindon at Blundell Park.

ginnywings: *OMG! The most entertaining game I've seen in many a moon. It had just about everything. Crosses, shots, flying saves, an incredible goal-line clearance, a worldy goal, a soft as shite goal, a come from behind win and a late winner. Even if the score had been reversed, I would have felt thoroughly entertained. Swindon played their part and made numerous chances but we made more and deserved the win.*

TO HELL AND BACK

We actually played football for large parts of the game and it was such a refreshing change from what has happened in previous games. I am still pinching myself, but well done to all, I didn't think they had it in them.

The Mariners then won at Barnet, often a happy hunting ground for them, on the Saturday. Six points in a week and five goals!

Barralad *A thoroughly comfortable win. A great defensive display to snuff out a toothless Barnet attack. On Tuesday the focus was on the switch of Davies to left back but no-one should underestimate the contribution of Zak Mills and his pace down the right.*

Collins and Clark reduced the formerly dangerous Akinde to a passenger. Summerfield largely ran midfield but Rose is growing in confidence and has more bite than Berrett.

D.J. was quieter than against Swindon but still gave Barnet plenty to think about.

Some of the interchanges involving Jones, Dembele and Matt reminded me at times of early Buckley days.

It was a great header by Matt for the first goal from a great delivery from Summerfield from a corner.

Now we come to Dembele. At times he was unplayable. He frightened Barnet to death and produced a fantastic run and slide rule pass to Jones for the second. He came in for some heavy treatment from players not fit to be on the same pitch with a thoroughly deserved straight red card for a two-footed tackle almost from behind. A week is a long time in football...

louth_in_the_south *Summerfield was everywhere today. An amazing transformation of a player who was consigned to the bin by many. Well done to him.*

forza ivano *Dunno what you lot on the Fishy were moaning about! They were bloody good, pacey, disciplined, hardworking and skilful. Summerfield was motm by a country mile, although Matt was excellent up front. Rose worked hard and the defence were very solid. Dembele is an absolute box of tricks, he's far too good for this level.*

[Barnet's] Akinde played a real captain's role, exemplary in his attitude, even at the end he was sprinting back 70 yards to snuff out an attack

WEEK 30

With no game in the last week of November the club decided to hold a fans' forum to try and settle some of the big issues which divided the fans and the board including: the boring style of play, the lukewarm response from the club to the events at Stevenage, the club's support of the Checkatrade trophy, the players Russell Slade had replaced, and the treatment of *Radio Humberside* journalist Matt Dean. Plus, the perennial topics of John Fenty's stranglehold over the club and his (many felt half-hearted) attempts to sell it. Not forgetting, of course, the new ground, which had dragged on for decades and seemed no closer. The evening by and large past peacefully during the part of the show aired on *Radio Humberside*. After that finished the debate continued (as can be seen on YouTube at https://www.youtube.com/watch?v=ueaC76mcsTs) and the room exploded over the subject of reporter Matt Dean, who was in the unfortunate position of hosting the debate!

HackneyHaddock I'm torn because on much of the substance (shares situation, efforts to find an investor, tax position, Bogle transfer, numbers around the stadium, honesty about JF's exit strategy) I thought the panel gave some clear answers.

Which brings us back to the style and presentation. If the club had bought in just a few days of training in how to handle media questions and handling/neutralising aggressive questioning, the same answers and facts could have been presented in a much better way and not poured petrol onto the fire.

Take Stephen Marley for example. He made a perfectly reasonable point that he'd spoken to a local HNWI about investing in the club and that this person was put off by the prospect of abuse from fans. I don't think anyone would dispute that as a plausible anecdote and wouldn't have expected him to divulge who it was. Matt Dean, as a journalist, did his job and asked Marley, at which point he exploded and started angrily bandying around phrases like "rank stupidity".

Why couldn't Marley have just said with a smile "Ha, nice try Matt and I understand you have to ask me that, as a journalist, but I'm sure you can appreciate I was asked to not divulge this person's identity and I'd like to keep my word to them. It does mean I'm asking you all to take me at my word on it, but because we're still involved in talking to people in business and football, it's also important that those we approach know they can trust us to act with discretion and keep confidences"

Why not just give that answer like any other professional would do, instead of kicking off like an episode of Jeremy Kyle?

Toontown*: That Steve Marley fellow came across as extremely arrogant and the epitome of why the club's PR is bad:*
- *complaining that fans should know his name (FFS!),*
- *that he didn't agree with the Checkatrade thing but because he thinks the money is right we all should too*
- *referring to money that was used to buy Bogle as not being from Operation Promotion and therefore the fans hadn't bought him when the vast majority of the club's income was of course from the fans*
- *his response to a BBC reporter who asked an obvious and straightforward question (that could and should have been so easily batted away)*
- *when asked a question not aimed at him but in reference to the whole board he took it upon himself to declare it had been aimed at him and was criticising him as 'not worthy' of a board seat (the questioner handled this very well and responded well IMO - and no it wasn't me lol)*
- *being unnecessarily abrasive and defensive throughout including saying fans thought he was a liar if they didn't accept his version of events re. investment. I actually thought his explanation was fine (albeit too long for some people's taste) and I personally believe him, I just don't think there was any need to "up the ante"' in that way and it was unhelpful.*

His behaviour and attitude were poor and unprofessional in my opinion, he seemed to be deliberately wanting to antagonise fans/the situation. I am not sure he would be the right person to represent the club in important dealings from what I have seen tonight.

Davmariner*: On behalf of anyone reasonable associated with GTFC, I apologise for the behaviour of our majority shareholder and manager at the fans forum. The right or wrongs of what went on aside, that sort of behaviour is embarrassing. If only those at the club were just as outraged at female fans having their bras searched...*

Meanwhile even on the Fishy tempers were short with long-time poster Grimsby Pete receiving a ban until the end of the year following his excessive number of posts about John Fenty on multiple threads. I was forced to defend the moderators' actions.

Lukea*: OK so I usually keep myself to myself and keep my personal life to myself but I'm currently going through a very fucking shit time and genuinely wake up some days wondering why I bother and whether I should just give up on life. It sounds stupid but something like the Fishy just gives people a little bit of a boost and smile. It may sound sad and pathetic to a lot but I* see where Pete is coming from. Being lonely isn't nice and haven't a shit real life isn't nice. Places like the Fishy give you a chance to take your mind off things and get your teeth stuck into something or gives you a smile when people type puns etc.

I hope Pete will be welcomed back soon, I'm not 100% sure what he's done or what was said but seeing things on here about his mental state etc. makes me feel like he needs this forum. I have always said a smile is infectious, a small please or thank you or holding a door for someone can go a long way. Every day you wake up and head to work and put a big brave smile on your face and hide the demons inside. It's not nice and not easy so I hope Pete is welcomed back sooner rather than later

GrimRob: How anybody can accuse this site of being pro-Fenty is beyond a joke when rarely an hour goes by without something critical of him appears on here! Its very name has become synonymous with anti-board posts.

John has barely communicated with me at all in the last couple of years and there has been no mention whatsoever of Pete in the communication that there has been between us. Occasionally we do have private words with people about their posts and generally, they are ok with it.

The Fishy has had and continues to have a very laissez-faire approach to posters and by and large just let everyone get on with it. Very few posts get reported using the button provided but when they do we'll always look at them. We get criticised when we do intervene and we get criticised when we don't. Like referees, you just can't keep all the people happy all the time.

What was needed after two weeks with no football and a prolonged period of infighting spread across the forum, Twitter and the infamous fans' forum was a game, and preferably a win to reignite the supporters into backing the team.

The last game seemed an eternity ago, but the League Table looked very healthy with Town just three points off the play-offs and the next game being at home to struggling Forest Green.

Pos	Team	P	W	D	L	F	A	GD	Pts
1	Luton	20	12	5	3	48	18	+30	41
2	Notts County	20	12	5	3	35	20	+15	41
3	Accrington	20	11	4	5	32	22	+10	37
4	Exeter	20	11	3	6	28	22	+6	36
5	Wycombe	20	9	6	5	38	29	+9	33
6	Coventry	20	9	5	6	21	12	+9	32
7	Mansfield	20	8	8	4	30	23	+7	32
8	Swindon	20	10	2	8	30	25	+5	32
9	Newport County	20	8	6	6	27	22	+5	30
10	Lincoln	20	8	6	6	24	19	+5	30
11	Colchester	20	8	5	7	26	23	+3	29
12	Grimsby	20	8	5	7	24	26	-2	29
13	Cambridge	20	8	5	7	17	23	-6	29
14	Carlisle	20	7	6	7	28	27	+1	27
15	Stevenage	20	7	5	8	26	31	-5	26
16	Cheltenham	20	6	6	8	27	29	-2	24
17	Crawley Town	20	5	6	9	17	23	-6	21
18	Yeovil	20	5	5	10	27	38	-11	20
19	Crewe	20	6	2	12	21	34	-13	20
20	Forest Green	20	5	5	10	23	39	-16	20
21	Morecambe	20	4	7	9	15	25	-10	19
22	Port Vale	20	5	3	12	19	31	-12	18
23	Barnet	20	4	5	11	21	29	-8	17
24	Chesterfield	20	4	5	11	23	37	-14	17

League Table 30th November

Rob Sedgwick

DECEMBER

Tough Opposition

WEEK 31

With no game on the club arranged a "Meet the Forwards" event, which won some rare praise for Town's goal-shy strikers.

> **Fishy_fishtails**: I was just wondering if many others went down with the kids this afternoon to meet some of the players? I took my offspring along, the club staff were very friendly and the players spent a fair amount of time chatting away with the younger generation. It was nice to see them off the pitch and getting involved. Well done to them. UTM.

But the backstabbing continued with John Fenty once again being accused, following some gaffe, of "Poor PR", seemingly his original sin.

> **RichMariner**: I worked in a PR team for a large business for 4 years and I am absolutely certain John Fenty doesn't know what PR is.
>
> He should know that in difficult times, PR is your most valuable weapon.
>
> When you're riding a crest of a wave, good PR can help you when bad days inevitably come along.
>
> Now, this next bit might seem harsh but I'm only pointing it out because something like this is on page 1 of the PR manual:

If you're going to make the effort to talk to the fans 'on a level', like one-to-one, great. But don't do it while perched on an expensive snooker table in your lavish home.

Fans cannot associate with that. You've got to make them feel like you're on their level, and not remind them of your different lifestyle. Why couldn't that interview be done behind closed doors at BP, i.e. a neutral venue that we can all associate with?

I don't want to ignite another thread discussing the same topic though.

I'll end with this: Public Relations isn't difficult. About 95% of it is common sense. Choosing the right time to say the right things, to the right people. But you've got to know what those people are thinking and feeling and understand their concerns.

If you haven't got the inclination to learn that last bit then you'll never make PR work for you.

Finally, after the long hiatus, December began with a 1-0 win over Forest Green which lifted Town level on points with the play-offs. It was the highest position achieved since Paul Hurst had left the club.

Arryarryarry: *Just back to the car, we played well first half, and played poorly second half. We didn't take advantage of the extra man.*

I couldn't understand the substitutions, Jones should give up the job of taking penalties.

But it's great to get three wins in a row.

The Old Codger: *I met Summers today (I have done his kit sponsorship) – he's a great lad with a really good attitude.*

Skrill: *Mitch Rose is turning into a solid box-to-box midfielder, he sealed 3 points against Crewe, sealed 3 points against Swindon and now against The Green Forest Village.*

With Town doing well, the Premier League vultures were starting to hover over Dembele (according to the papers).

KingstonMariner: I think this is irresponsible journalism. There's probably some poor midfielder at Swansea (or Palace) worrying about his job now.

Finally, the criticism was getting too much for some fans, especially giving the team were doing quite well position-wise.

HotToddy: Some might find this hard to believe. The vast majority of Town fans go to a game, support their team, then go home.

WEEK 32

More off the field controversy when the much-praised and popular SLO quit, despite the accolades after Bragate, and was replaced by an in-house appointment.

Director John Fenty once again came on the site to explain circumstances, which was greeted with the predictable backlash.

JF: It's a grey area that clearly needs to be reconciled. To avoid the need for another official statement about this I'll seek to defuse the hysteria by the following.

On the one hand, Kristen who has done some great work, often speaks on behalf of the Trust with no reference to the Club ('Bragate' the prime example where her last statement called for the club to condemn the EFL) Who was she speaking working for then?

There were originally 3 SLO officers which reduced down to one almost without notice, an earlier link [on the site] highlights the arrangement and the Trust's nomination.

The Club have 'listened' and are putting in place a club appointed SLO who is available every day and works for the Club in very important areas such as Disability and Inclusion to help to close the gap, or, perceived gap between the Club and its supporters.

In the following link [on the club's IFollow], Adie speaking gives a clear insight and his desire to work with Kristine and the Role.

This confusion needs clearing up about who Kristine reports to and what are their joint terms of reference and the basis for how messages coming out from them which must have the clearance of the Club.

It's a very important role and I hope everyone will join me in welcoming Adie on board.

Best Wishes John F

ska face: *Where do you start with this latest fucking skip fire from the desk of Lord J.S. Fenty (Con)?*

Unless I'm mistaken, the SLO role, a great opportunity to give fans a say in the club and in shaping supporter experience, was initially handed to Sue Mullen, wife of then-director Lee Mullen. When questions were raised about why, and indeed how, this happened, the club backtracked and added two additional roles (one for disabled supporter liaison and one working with charities, for some reason). Essentially this demonstrates not only a misunderstanding of the role itself and the potential benefits of having someone in place, it raises yet more questions about GTFC's recruitment procedures and does nothing to dispel fears of the "jobs for the boys" culture at the club.

You're right, there are grey areas in the current management of the SLO role and where exactly it sits - perhaps someone should have thought about this before? If only there were people at the club paid to make such decisions. We can but dream.

However, the work that Kristine Green has done in the role - alongside the Mariners Trust who have assisted and supported the development of the role - has surely surpassed all expectations, often going above and beyond for the benefit of FANS. And that is the problem - the role in its current format had the fans' interests at heart, and the GTFC board couldn't give a fiddler's fuck about fans, their well-being or their "experience".

No better example of this could have been asked for than "Bragate", where a number of fans were effectively subjected to sexual assault at worst and gross invasion of personal space at best. Where were GTFC in all of this? Nowhere. Shite it. They did nothing for these fans who travel the length and breadth of the country to support their team. When did we hear from GTFC? Only when their staff were implicated. The fans that are so pilloried by yourself and others, at any given opportunity, that your ludicrous statements have been reported by the country's largest news outlet, were abandoned.

So, when the SUPPORTERS needed a SUPPORTER LIAISON OFFICER, Kristine and The Trust not only supported us but also raised awareness of this issue excellently amongst the rest of the football league and beyond. What did the club do? Nothing. Covered their arses and left the fans to their own get on with it. The less said about the way you have used this as a stick to beat The Trust with recently, the better, as you're past the point of embarrassing yourself.

So let's move on. You note that you've "listened". Listened to fucking who?! Who, ever, has said that the club needs ANOTHER SLO? When? If that is the sum total of what you took from the fans' forum and debates on here then...Christ, we really are in trouble. The role of the SLO is to give fans an active say in their matchday experience and the opportunity to feed in and be listened to. We already have that - we have that in an existing SLO and, you may not have noticed this, we also have a representative from the Mariners Trust on the board of directors. If you wanted to listen, try listening to these two, who are already doing Adie's job for him. Though I suppose this is yet more evidence that you won't listen to the fans - you may hear us, but you certainly don't listen.

One of the benefits of an SLO is that it opens up a clear, demonstrable chain of communication between the fans and the club. We know who to talk to, about what, and who hears this message. Now what? We've got two SLO's, one handed a job by you with seemingly no experience of the issues fans face at places like Stevenage, at Doncaster, Notts County and other places that the current SLO had demonstrated her worth. Who do we raise concerns with now? Do we trust GTFC to act on these concerns raised with the new SLO? I can only speak for myself here, but I wouldn't trust someone put in place by you, unnecessarily, as yet another buffer, to deliver any meaningful, positive change for the good of the fans. The disdain with which you and other GTFC staff treat fans is clear, and I won't be expecting anything new from yet another internal appointment. Trust is key to the role of the SLO, and there'll have to be some big steps taken to build that from your current position.

YET AGAIN, this is another opportunity to build on some good work initially done by The Trust which GTFC have pissed up a wall. Fan engagement and the "matchday experience" is absolutely critical to encouraging new fans and retaining them, especially with a new stadium supposedly on the horizon that you'll need to fill. Does this announcement give the impression that you particularly care? Not to me. Does it show you know what you're doing? I'll let others answer that.

What it does demonstrate, quite clearly, is that you can't bear to have anyone take a shred of power from you. You talk about how statements and comments need to be cleared by the club - that's fucking rich coming from you! How many of YOUR statements are cleared by the rest of the board, including the other major shareholder in the club, the Mariners Trust? In fact, where they (as in WE) even consulted on this change?

I'm sure Adie's a nice guy, and good luck to him in this ~~already existing~~ new role, but as a fan, I'm expecting nothing other than another mouthpiece for the board's bad decisions. What a fucking mess. Again.

Chrisblor: *John Fenty is killing our club. He's a vacuous, vain and arrogant man who holds us all in contempt. We must force him out. We had one of the best SLOs in the country, but did he care about that? Of course not. A total shame to lose Kristine, and a shameful affair all round.*

Nevertheless, the staff in the club shop won some rare praise notwithstanding the maelstrom of criticism directed "upstairs".

Shilts: *Thought this deserved a thread. In light of all the negativity off the pitch and the club getting 'pilloried' so much, today I experienced something that they have got very right.*

I took the kids down the club shop today for the crafts on offer, tree decorations and stone painting.

I have to say it exceeded all expectations. It was really well prepared, really well run and could not have been made more welcome by all staff in the club shop. The kids were delighted and one extra fan was gained as even the football hating wife said it made her feel as though the club should be supported (bless her she doesn't know about all the other stuff).

Anyway, big well done to all involved in organising and running this. Shows some things can get done right.

After the three wins Town had three tough games against Notts County, Luton and Mansfield to come, and things continued to look hopeful after a battling 0-0 draw at leaders Notts County.

Barralad *A very entertaining 0-0 draw with Town probably just on top overall. I expected better from County who seemed content to launch long balls to Ameobi who was handled very well by Clark and Collins. The only real chance was from Summerfield's deflected effort in the* first half although I'm not sure how their 'keeper ended up with the ball in his hands in a goalmouth melee in the first period.

There was a bit of a heart in mouth moment when Macca careered out of his goal to bring down their lad who was going away from goal.

Man of the Match....by an absolute country mile Summerfield. Energy, commitment, decent dead ball delivery and some crisp passing. Superb!!!

Despite the point, the drunken Town fans at the game in Nottingham invited much criticism.

Freemoash88: Well yesterday we had it all. Chief inspectors telling their minions to round up anybody wearing any sort of Stone Island clothing whilst letting the real idiots walk off so they can start on young County lads. Idiots walking around Nottingham shouting racist remarks as well as "get your tits out" to women walking past. Over the top bouncers outsider boozers.

To top it all off fans arguing and nearly scrapping inside the ground because one section was shouting Fenty out whilst the other was telling them to shut up and get behind the team. Plus certain Town fans having a pop at any Town player that did the slightest thing wrong. I had 5 wankers behind me having a pop at Ben Davies all game.

I love away games but fuck me we do have some right cunts.

GYinScuntland: Five of our scrotes thought I was Notts and went for me.
Five eighteen or twenty-year-olds onto a single fifty eight-year-old.
Well done cunts.
They still backed off when given it back.
Cocks.
A van of Old Bill passed and tried not to notice as well.

cod_head_doug: My wife and I travel to all the away games. Following the final whistle at Barnet, we were very aggrieved to find that the Ladies toilets were locked, which we took great exception to. We remonstrated with the stewards and were told to use Starbucks.

The next day my wife e-mailed Barnet football club and made a formal complaint. We have now received a reply that the reason the toilets were locked was that during the match somebody had daubed excrement over the walls and they had to deep clean them.

TO HELL AND BACK

At Notts County my wife went to the Ladies at halftime and found one of the toilet seats smashed off and urine all over the place. Now I don't believe this was done by our female supporters, so the only conclusion is that some of our male fans are using and abusing the female facilities at away fixtures.

If this is indeed the case, then I really do despair, no wonder we are treated so badly at some grounds.

The shame on our Club's reputation and indeed our Town's.

Act like animals and you get treated like animals, while the decent supporters get tarred with the same brush!

The point had the optimists getting their calculators out.

Mariner55: *After that good point at Notts County on Saturday I had a look at historic League Two tables to get an idea of how many points we would need to get into the play-offs and how many to avoid relegation.*

Based on the last seven seasons, the lowest total of points required to get into the play-offs was 68 (2010-2011). The highest was 75 in 2015-2016.

The highest number of points a relegated team got was 51 in 2012-2013, followed by 50 the next season. In 2015-2016 the second to bottom (ie also relegated) team got just 34 points.

We're currently running at 1.5 points/game, so at this rate would get 69 points - probably not enough to get into the play-offs but with the recent improved form, who knows. I reckon we need another 20 to be safe.

All a bit of fun ... please feel free to attack me now.

WEEK 33

The club once again issued a statement about Matt Dean, they seemingly just couldn't let it lie. The backlash on The Fishy was of course inevitable.

BP Vicar: Those at the club have a high opinion of themselves. Much ado about nothing IMO, we're only a tinpot 4th division outfit. Matt will more likely be around long after RS and JF have gone. Keep asking questions Matt, RH is independent and must not become another mouthpiece of the club.

Civvy at last: What I really don't get is that if Slade invited Woodhouse and knew the full reason for him being there, which is what he said at the forum. How could he possibly be worried about his job, when the source is a dodgy tweet??

The whole thing doesn't make sense to me and a lot of other folk too.

arryarryarry: If anyone on here or the players or Russell Slade thought that John Fenty was going to replace RS with Curtis Woodhouse whose managerial highlights are managing Sheffield FC and Goole Town in the Northern Premier League then they are complete and utter fuckwits.

headingly_mariner: The club are making a mess of this. I think there was some truth in what Matt was tweeting in first place. The suggestion out of Brid is that Woodhouse thought he was moving on.

If Russell Slade had allowed him to come and watch training why would he and the players think he'd been sacked for Woodhouse to replace him?

Our club deals in alternative facts and fake news, you only have to look at what the club put out about the SLO appointment and compare it with Kristine's statement to question the accuracy of the information coming from the club.

The 0-0 draw at Notts County was followed by a 2-0 defeat at Luton, another side near the top of the table, so not regarded as a great shock.

barralad: Town were beaten by a better side today. Luton's passing and movement reminded me at times of Town in Buckley's first spell. It may well however have been very different if their lad had received the correct colour card for scything down Dembele in front of the dugout. It was late, his feet were off the floor and he wasn't in control. Textbook straight red really!

For 40 odd minutes Town defended as well as they did at County last week but then the midfield parted with one pass leaving their guy to curl an unstoppable effort inside the post. Macca had no chance.

To their credit Town continued to battle with Sam Jones involved in most of the attacking stuff although in truth our lack of a cutting edge was demonstrated again and again. Summerfield fired one just wide first half and Matt hit the outside of the post from a very tight angle early second half.

The second goal killed the game really with their lad getting in front of our defender (I couldn't see who) from a free kick.

Once D.J. and Siriki departed the flair also went. Hooper played some useful link-up play, Vernon did what he always does, put the effort in but we never really looked like giving them a nervy last 20.

MOTM was a toss up between Clarke and Collins (unless either were the defender sleeping for goal number 2.)

Good turn out of by the Mariners who made plenty of noise.

I'll be amazed if Luton aren't automatically promoted on their showing today.

WEEK 34

Christmas, it was fair to say was not a merry one for Town supporters. The wheels came off the promotion train with just 1 point to show for the four festive games, a 1-1 draw on Boxing Day.

Town drew against Mansfield at Blundell Park on Boxing Day, and keeper James McKeown limped off midway through the game to be replaced by rookie Ben Killip. They were slipping down the table, but Mansfield *were* one of the stronger sides.

Hagrid The ref's decision to book Matt for absolutely fuck all ruined the game, his decision to not give a pen at the end was a disgrace considering his decision to blow at every slight tug and nudge anywhere. He bottled sending off the RB in the 1st half and he cost us 3 points as our subs just offered nothing, but I don't blame Slade as he had to make them.

Alfi It's crazy how differently people can see a game. I thought it was Dembele's best game for Town today. When will Clarke start getting some praise? The first month aside - he has been outstanding and was a rock today.

We're a striker away from being play-off contenders - Matt either needs an on-it Jones or someone to run in behind for him. The difference in confidence between Killip and another young goalkeeper in Henderson was stark. He made a couple of saves but looked like he was shitting himself. You could see Evans told them to get at him second half

---

The 3-0 defeat at home to Accrington was a stark indication how far off the pace Town were in this league.

---

devs Accrington attacked as a pack - 4/5 going forward, great movement, pinpoint passing, clinical finishing - everything we weren't.

They have some very good 'footballers' - and I don't mean 6ft 3in lumps who are athletes first and footballers second.

Player who are encouraged to get the ball down and pass it

This is what you get with hoof ball I'm afraid - no tactical acumen, no joined-up thinking when the 'big fella' knocks it down, and players who don't know what to do when they get a sniff of a chance

Slade's football HAS to be successful because there is no aesthetic enjoyment - a few wins here and there just paper over the cracks and eventually it fails

It's the PL equivalent of Pulis at WBA - once their slide started the ugliness of the football just comes to the fore and fans vote with their mouths and feet

It's odd because 6pts off play-offs and mid-table security is not the worst place to be – but the whole package (off and on field) feels as bad as I can remember.

I've never felt less of a connection with a GTFC team/set up as this in 35 years of supporting them – it feels so characterless and devoid of any enjoyment

May 2016 and Wembley seems like light years away

BP Vicar. *Worryingly I saw plenty of effort. Sam Jones, what on earth is wrong with him? Offside twice in the first half from kicks from our goalkeeper, he turned into trouble all the time. Zak Mills seemed to be limping throughout the game, yet he stayed on, even at 3-0 down. We have no pace in the side, and offer nothing up front. JJ Hooper had a good chance, but somehow fell over – he's awful, DJ doesn't know when to release the ball, he seems to play for himself. Matt is our best centre-forward and he's a touch like a donkey, it says it all.*

We are a very poor side, and we're going backwards again. I've had enough of this excrement. Please go JF, it's time for someone else to have a go.

denni266. *The match was a total shambles from start to finish. Slade has no idea, get gone and take Fenty with you*

The drubbing at Blundell Park to their unfancied opponents was the final straw for some Town fans. There was only one man to blame.

Theimperialcoroner. *Slade has been utterly shown up so far today. Zero clue. The players are instructed to play percentage football and they have no idea what to do if it's not working. There are no options from the bench and no vision on the field. It's miles off good enough and I can't remember such a shocking performance.*

Get the bald one out now. Stop the Sludge.

Meanwhile the news that Jamie Osborne was staying at Solihull, where he had been on loan, even though Town's midfield had been so awful recently, was treated with dismay. Osborne had been one of the better players of 2016-2017 but had barely had a chance this season.

BP Vicar. *What an absolute mug I am for believing him and the club about it only being a one-month loan so he can build fitness. He's staying at a shite little club, something's gone on there. Scandalous, whatever's gone on, he needs to get his arse back to Grimsby, whether or not he has self-imposed 'transport' issues or not, get in a B&B, take responsibility and do the job you've been signed for and are being paid for.*

Maybe I'm being unfair here, but I'm hearing things and it's a joke.

headingly_mariner. *He got a 2 1/2 year deal, he should have moved to the area. There is no way we should've signed players on long contracts who weren't willing to move to within an hour of the area.*

The league table was not great, but it was not terrible either. Town were far closer to the play-offs than they were the relegation zone. But they seemed way off the standard of the top teams, judging by the results in December. The previous 18 months had been almost constant mid-table inconsistency. The rest of the season at this stage looked to be more of the same, unless of course the elusive goalscorer was signed in the January transfer window.

Pos	Team	P	W	D	L	F	A	GD	Pts
1	Luton	25	15	6	4	58	23	+35	51
2	Notts County	25	13	8	4	43	26	+17	47
3	Lincoln	25	12	7	6	33	20	+13	43
4	Exeter	24	13	3	8	34	30	+4	42
5	Coventry	25	12	5	8	27	18	+9	41
6	Wycombe	25	11	7	7	44	34	+10	40
7	Accrington	24	12	4	8	38	30	+8	40
8	Colchester	25	11	7	7	35	27	+8	40
9	Mansfield	25	10	10	5	35	28	+7	40
10	Swindon	24	12	2	10	36	33	+3	38
11	Newport County	25	9	9	7	33	29	+4	36
12	Cambridge	25	10	6	9	25	31	-6	36
13	Carlisle	25	9	7	9	36	34	+2	34
14	Grimsby	25	9	7	9	26	32	-6	34
15	Cheltenham	25	8	7	10	32	34	-2	31
16	Port Vale	25	9	4	12	29	33	-4	31
17	Stevenage	25	8	6	11	32	38	-6	30
18	Crawley Town	25	8	6	11	23	30	-7	30
19	Yeovil	25	7	6	12	35	45	-10	27
20	Crewe	25	8	2	15	27	41	-14	26
21	Morecambe	25	6	7	12	24	36	-12	25
22	Chesterfield	25	5	6	14	26	46	-20	21
23	Barnet	25	5	5	15	25	37	-12	20
24	Forest Green	24	5	5	14	24	45	-21	20

League Table 31st December

Grimsby had, to be fair, been playing the top teams and the matches at the beginning of 2018 were mainly against the teams at the other end of the table. The expectation was that Town would start to pick up points again against these "lesser" teams and at very least establish themselves in a comfortable mid-table position.

Rob Sedgwick

JANUARY

The Collapse

WEEK 35

Town did not have a happy new year, losing 2-0 at Crewe, which virtually put paid to any lingering hope of making the play-offs.

Lincspoacher: I should have listened to the Mrs when suggested to son we go today!

I won't repeat some accurate observations about how we played today from previous posts. However, as an ex-player I can tell that half the side did not want to be there today. The body language was defeatist, negative and absolutely no leadership in the team as well as the obvious technical deficiencies already commented on.

I am 100% certain that RS does not have a squad fighting or believing in what he is trying to do.

It's one thing to have absolutely no threat in front of goal, which we do. But coupled with a team that has lost its desire, then these are perilous weeks for us as a real nosedive is possible.

I see real problems ahead and let's be honest, we can keep changing our managers but the issues at GTFC are much deeper and more fundamental than that.

The club has a leadership crisis from top to bottom, a culture of blame and bullying when challenged and a complete lack of transparency and humility from its board.

Worrying times.

Grimsby Pete, the Fishy's most prolific poster was allowed back after a few weeks of being banned from the forum.

> **grimsby pete**: Hi guys I am back and would like to thank all the ones who spoke up for me when I was suspended.
>
> The football has gone down the drain since I last posted.
>
> BUT :)
>
> I will try and see a few of you at Colchester seeing my op has been cancelled for another month (bloody government)
>
> You never know I might be a lucky charm and we will see a Town goal !!!!!!!
>
> It's good to be back.

It got worse on the Saturday when Grimsby lost 2-0 at Blundell Park at home to Morecambe, a match which the previous season had been Town's first since returning the Football League. It was a far cry from that sunny day, when Town had started the new campaign with three points and Paul Hurst had made his debut as a league manager.

> **Hagrid**: That was one of the worst performances I can ever remember seeing. Gutless passionless embarrassing woeful plus many more. It must end now. Go to the dressing room Fenty and sack Slade, sack Wilko, and then walk yourself. I don't care if I'm not supposed to say this, I'm a fan, you're a stranglehold of this club. And we, the fans, have had enough. You have taken away every single jot of joy I got after promotion. We are in real, real trouble courtesy of your mate Slade. All GO now as we cannot and will not go on like this.

Midfielder Chris Clements returned from his loan spell at Barrow and immediately was accused of being fat by one poster who won the derision of most of the regulars.

ginnywings: *Well that's a lovely welcome back I must say. It was reported that he had some personal problems, so can't we just cut him some slack? He was decent for us last season I thought.*

WEEK 36

Town had started the year with three straight losses and made it four with another home defeat, this time to Newport. It was the third successive home defeat and the natives were getting even more restless than usual.

Gaffer58: *Just Back. Somebody should contact the NSPCC, making kids watch that, they could be scared for life.*

No way was there that many [3397] today the Main Stand was virtually empty. The Upper Findus was empty. In no way were there more there today than last week. Was this done deliberately because they knew fans would vote with their feet?

The board had to respond, and they did, with a vote of confidence in manager Russell Slade. The end was surely nigh?

Link:https://www.grimsbytelegraph.co.uk/sport/football/grimsby-town-board-vote-stick-1034764

ginnywings: *Does anyone think Slade should stay? After my rantings of last week, I decided to just sit back and see what happens in the Window. The club made their statement and I thought, ok, let's see what you do, over to you. But I do worry about the direction we are heading and can see similarities to when we fell out of the league, so will air my thoughts on this.*

I think it's more important to look at the appointment to begin with. The club must have known (and if they didn't, they should have) that the hiring of Slade would be massively divisive and that he wouldn't be afforded the same leeway as another manager would simply because of his past. We now have a manager who is deeply unpopular and is losing games too, which is an untenable position. I think it's more than likely we will lose the next 2 games as well and the pressure will just keep ratcheting up. I don't think I have heard manager out chants so quickly in a tenure as this one. All I hear at every game is, "we shouldn't have brought him back" and I think the board, not for the first time, have totally misjudged the fans' feelings.

I also think it was a lazy appointment. The board decided for good or bad that Bignot had to go and from the rumblings we have heard, it seems he was causing havoc behind the scenes, so fair enough. We are safe in the league and have the rest of the season to find the right guy. But it is now apparent that instead of sacking Bignot and then looking for a new manager, the manager being available was the reason Bignot went when he did. A 'perfect' solution was there for the taking as far as the board were concerned and Slade could come in with no pressure and spend the rest of the season assessing the squad. I think the appointment of Wilko was to assuage the fans and I very much doubt he was requested by Slade. He looks like he was shoehorned into the job and I have no knowledge of him ever doing anything of note in the game on the management side anywhere else. Subsequent signings of players linked to Wilko's past have largely been a complete dud, so one has to ask about his role in all this too. In short, the club have got it wrong again I am afraid to say.

So where do we go from here? I'm certain that JF will be running all this through his head right now and I don't envy him. Do you stick, or do you twist when the future of the football club is once again on the line? It should never have got to this stage, but somehow at GTFC, it always does.

The Old Codger: *I question the sanity of the board of GTFC! If the manager who you appointed and have now backed can seriously state that we didn't deserve to lose today, then either I need my eyes testing or he is an utter bullshitter. With him in charge, we will either get relegated this season or next.*

WEEK 37

Grimsby grabbed a point at Colchester in a 1-1 draw, which won Russell Slade a bit more time at least, but didn't stop Town's slide down the table.

HistonMariner: Just Back. In the first half, as has largely been said, we played better than all of us there probably expected. Of course, there was a lot of concern and even nervousness but Town got off to a flyer and played some good stuff. Matt and Vernam linked up to provide some real hope. Summerfield continued his worthy efforts to drive Town forward and I have to say (red cross if you must) I thought Dixon looked O.K. If we had gone in 2/3 up at half-time there could have been no complaints.

Cynically you could say, "But we weren't 2/3 up!", "We were playing a rubbish team", "If he'd picked X or Y we would have won."

Second Half: They obviously had a half-time bollocking and came out a different team. I was disappointed when we conceded that the body language seemed to portray negative vibes - I suppose this is about confidence but Summerfield appeared the only one to be trying to rouse the others. I think we need more leaders on the pitch. However, Town held up and Vernam had a great effort from the edge of the box that rattled the bar near the end.

It is about confidence. It is about momentum. It is about a bit of luck. All cliché I know.

We can talk of leadership from the top. We can talk of Management. We can talk of engagement etc etc.

BUT I am trying (at this point) to talk about today and the team.
Next week is Luton and that might spark a different conversation............ In the meantime, UTMM

The Vera: My dream last night was quite surreal I dreamt I was slowly being choked to death whilst watching Town failing miserably at Blundell Park. The focus of my dream seemed to be Woolford who was particularly inept but then he was substituted for Jaiyesimi. From that point on Town slowly got the upper hand and all the life returned to my body.

In summary last night a DJ saved my life.

January was almost over, and Town were now about due to sack the manager, rotten timing considering how bad the squad seemed to be.

Mariner9t *Let's face it, he'll not be going for at least the next two games and we'll sack him just after the Window slams shut. It will be the absolutely worst timing possible but then that's what happens when you've got a board full of clowns.*

LH *I've got a scam season ticket for a football ground but they don't play football etc etc.*

The bookies at this stage were confident that Grimsby would stay up. You could get 50/1 on Grimsby being relegated. It looked, frankly, a good bet.

WEEK 38

But normal service was resumed when Grimsby once more lost at Blundell Park, despite Luton playing nearly the whole game with ten men.

Mimma *Same old, same old.*

We actually played alright, but lack of pace and movement up front cost us. We don't get the ball forward quick enough, and don't try to get behind or down the wings to stretch them. You can change the players around to your heart's content, but if we don't change the way we play we are never going to score. Too predictable. Summerfield hit the bar from twenty-five yards, Matt just missed the target, but the longer it went on the less likely we were to score. I was disappointed in Luton, and their support (522!).

The player who was sent off needs a brain transplant: a very bad tackle for the first booking, a knee-high challenge for the second. Stupid. They sat back after the sending off. If Summerfield's effort had gone in it would have been a lot different.

We need to change the whole style of play, and that can only happen when the manager is changed.

Freemoash88 *Not sure if the young lad [Killip] reads this but just wanted to say you gave a good performance yesterday. Your kicking distribution was great and on one occasion you might have got an assist with that long kick down to Vernam who went through on goal. You* *pulled off a couple of good saves and that save from the free-kick where you tipped it onto the bar was top class. It wasn't your fault their players were more alert.*

Keep it up lad your doing great, don't let your head drop.

The after-match comments of Russell Slade continued to rile the fans who every week heard the same bad luck tales from him.

---

ginnywings: *I am listening to Slade as I type. You are so deluded mate. Ask yourself how many shots their keeper had to save, even against ten men?*

I can't be arsed to type any more. I am sick of it all.

Hagrid: *He is an arrogant, deluded, rude fool. We are in serious shit. Fucking "no luck". Fuck off Slade they had 10 men for an hour!!!!! Please John, I beg again, sack him and sack Wilkinson.*

Meanwhile there was hope that Slade had finally gone

---

crusty ole pie: *I got back into town at 19:30 and the floodlights were still on I wondered if there was a public hanging taking place.*

Mallyner: *Luton have gone home and we are still trying to score :)*

The board continued to receive lots of advice most of which was to sack Russell Slade, or words to that effect.

Grimsbys finest: *I honestly think that the board are thinking that this feeling amongst the supporters will blow over. Sadly, the club is going to be in for a big shock when season ticket sales half. I know attendances are holding up at the moment but that's mainly due to season ticket holders turning up and hoping they are going to get a shock and be entertained. If results* go against us then we will be 18 points behind a play-off spot. I would say give a manager time to experiment but if we don't pick up 6 points from the next 3 games then we are in serious trouble, looking at our remaining games. Please John, for the sake of the club's future you need to sack him. I know he is your friend but the facts are that he has been in the job for 20 years and never had a promotion, he has failed at his previous three clubs and his recruitment has been horrendous. One of the worrying parts about it is that he doesn't seem to have a solution to the problems on the pitch and he continues to say phrases such as "we must be positive" (how can this be when you have won 1 game in 9 matches) and "we know this group of players can score goals as we have done it in the past" (we have the worst goal scoring record in the league). I have a horrible feeling that the board may have given him a ridiculous contract and we can't afford to pay him off which is a worry, you gave him your vote of confidence 3 games ago and the facts are staring you right in the face. Please act now John as the loyalty of the fans will not remain if we drop down to the Conference again.*

WEEK 39

Town's last chance to win in January was a midweek game away at Yeovil, one of the most ridiculous fixtures of the season. But 129 away supporters turned up to watch Town lose 3-0.

Theimperialcoroner. *It was clueless from start to finish. Rose probably deserved to go, but their player was a disgrace. The ref chose to show cards rather than managing the game, but we made it easy for him to look like a branch of Clinton's. Some players are nowhere near good enough and some are going through the motions. Most though tried and they are being forced to play anti-football. They are scared of the ball and scared of making a mistake. This is entirely within the gift of the manager to fix. He's incapable though. Can you imagine Buckley tolerating such a state of affairs? Slade hid at the end which tells you all you need to know about this useless, classless arsehole.*

Bristol Mariner. *Just back in a wet Bristol so thankfully not too far to travel! I feel sorry for the players if I'm honest, they looked distraught at the end when they came over. At least Bignot had the balls to apologise at Crewe to the fans, let alone walk over. Dave Moore on Sat - 1,000 extra on the gate and a battle!*

With the transfer window closing top-scorer Sam Jones joined Shrewsbury, linking up with former boss Paul Hurst.

---

ginnywings: *I'm fucking fuming at this. You said you would bring in quality and not only have you not done that, you have let the only quality players we had left leave. It's symptomatic of the shitshow that is GTFC, we are losing our best player to Shrewsbury fooking Town.*

Slade is acting like a despot, ridding the entire previous regime from the history books. If we have three better players than Sam Jones, Chris Clement and Jamey Osborne left on the books, then I'm a fucking Martian.

headingly_mariner: *There's something very wrong about the whole situation with Jones. He looked comfortably our best player until a loss of form in recent months. He was the only one capable of hitting the net with any sort of regularity and needed working with to improve. He was the one capable of 20 goals in this division. He struck me as being a bit of a sulky twat, but that's where a manager needs to manage.*

It's a huge gamble to take selling your biggest goal threat when you can't score.

The statement the other week was clearly hot air. Fenty Out.

With former manager Paul Hurst's team flying high in League One, it was inevitable that fans contrasted his new club Shrewsbury with the one he left behind.

KingstonMariner *(replying to another post): It's not him [Hurst] I'm blaming [for leaving]. How did this come to pass, eh? We should have been closing the gap on these, historically smaller clubs. And go check the population of Shrewsbury. Surrounded by countryside.*

We should have been building on promotion 18 months ago. Crowds were up, we were heading in the right direction, we were solvent, now look at us. Complete reversal. Fucked about getting rid of managers after a few months. Failed yet again to market season tickets. Pissed off the fanbase two seasons running by supporting the Checkatwat. Kept quiet when fans were mistreated at Stevenage. Made nonsensical announcement after nonsensical announcement. Engineered a highly respected SLO out of the position that you'd appointed her to (yet somehow 'think' she works for another organisation). Treated the host of the forum with disrespect and acted unprofessionally. Select as developers of the new stadium a no-mark bunch of posh skateboarders who insult your supporters. Keep your mate in the post despite his recruitment and retention policy being blatantly aimed at shipping out talent and on-boarding journeymen. Allowed players out on loan to rivals in the scrap to avoid relegation.

Fenty sling your hook. You've fucked us up once with non-league football. Now it's happening again. You've cost us far more than the 'benign' loans you've made. Accept you're a failure at running a football club before you totally wreck it.

Clements also left, joining Forest Green on loan until the end of the season. Town seemed to be offloading their best players long before the 50-point safety margin had been reached.

FishFan101 *Strengthening a relegation rival at this stage of the season is absolutely bonkers.*

Messages flooded in directed at the board.

RexFannies *John, Russell. We existed before you and will do long after.*

I remember my Newman's Aces scarf; the Drinkell hat-trick against Sheffield United; living next door to Dave Boylen and being too young to take advantage of it. I remember watching in disbelief as we crushed Man City 4-1 at Blundell Park and John Cockerill's determination in beating Exeter to win promotion. I remember Wayne Burnett scoring at Wembley and causing Alan Buckley's massive hip thrust. Winning at 2-1 Anfield; losing 5-0 at Anfield. I remember Turf Moor against Burnley to get to the Auto Windscreen cup final; beating West Ham 3-0 after drawing at their place. Beating Fulham in the play-offs. Shearers Lip; Kalala's goal. Paul Peschisolido's tackle on Handyside. Wilko's goal versus Everton. Tony Ford. Mick Brolly scoring twice against Everton. Dave Beasant being called "Butterfingers" on Calendar and beating Newcastle in their own backyard - Jim Dobbin. The Town versus WBA grudge games and the way Groves hit that penalty. Ivano Bonetti scoring at Tranmere. Thousands travelling to Plough Lane with their Harry Haddocks. The 6-5 win over Burnley. The 7-1 defeat to Sheffield Wednesday. Paul Futcher tackling someone with his head. Super Clive Mendonca. The slowest goal in the world by Big Keith. The whole ground singing "You only sing when you're winning" to Scunthorpe after coming from a goal down to win 2-1. Neil Woods's 2-goal debut at Preston on a plastic pitch, Neil Woods as manager. Travelling to Portsmouth and being 4-0 down at halftime. Buckley 1,2 and 3. Standing in the Barrett stand and watching the reserves. I remember Doug Everitt and Bryan Huxford. I remember being top of League 1. The Championship. Finishing 5th in what would now be the Championship. I remember being bottom, being down and being out. Chasetown. A never to be bettered team goal against Huddersfield in the 5-1 drubbing. It's Birtles on the back page of the Telegraph. I remember Bill Carr as Chairman. I remember it being great and I remember it being terrible. The bad times were only bad because of the good times.

*I cannot **ever** remember it being all bad. Until Now. That is what you have done.*

Meanwhile the Town players at least showed their humanity.

***Sigone**: Luke Summerfield tweeted earlier that Feb is going to be a great month.*

I replied: got to be better than January, I didn't see us win a game and I lost my dad. Things can only get better. Good luck Saturday.

Luke responded: Sorry to hear about your loss. Pass on my best wishes to you and your family. Hope for a great end to the season and win Saturday for you and your Dad.

I thought I would share this to prove players do have a heart and to be honest it meant a lot to me and would have meant a lot to my dad.

Town's prospects of promotion had entirely disappeared. While fans were starting to look downwards rather than upwards, the gap between Grimsby and the bottom two was still substantial and there were quite a few teams perched in between them and the relegation zone. No need to panic?

Pos	Team	P	W	D	L	F	A	GD	Pts
1	Luton	30	18	6	6	66	30	+36	60
2	Wycombe	29	15	7	7	55	40	+15	52
3	Notts County	29	14	9	6	48	32	+16	51
4	Exeter	28	16	3	9	40	33	+7	51
5	Coventry	29	15	5	9	34	21	+13	50
6	Mansfield	29	13	11	5	43	32	+11	50
7	Swindon	29	16	2	11	45	40	+5	50
8	Accrington	28	15	4	9	48	34	+14	49
9	Lincoln	29	13	9	7	41	28	+13	48
10	Newport County	30	12	10	8	41	36	+5	46
11	Colchester	30	11	10	9	40	37	+3	43
12	Crawley Town	30	12	6	12	32	35	-3	42
13	Carlisle	29	11	8	10	39	37	+2	41
14	Stevenage	30	10	8	12	38	41	-3	38
15	Cambridge	29	10	8	11	28	39	-11	38
16	Cheltenham	30	9	8	13	40	45	-5	35
17	Grimsby	31	9	8	14	28	43	-15	35
18	Port Vale	30	9	6	15	34	41	-7	33
19	Yeovil	29	8	7	14	41	50	-9	31
20	Morecambe	30	7	9	14	29	41	-12	30
21	Crewe	29	9	2	18	34	49	-15	29
22	Chesterfield	30	7	6	17	30	53	-23	27
23	Forest Green	30	7	5	18	31	53	-22	26
24	Barnet	29	5	7	17	28	43	-15	22

League Table 31st Jan

Rob Sedgwick

FEBRUARY

Journey to the Bottom of the League

WEEK 39 (CONTINUED)

With everyone expecting a sacking any day, Russell Slade once more got the backing of the board. The Town boss hit back at the critics with claims that he was building for the future and the fans should be patient and give him time. The idea was quickly rubbished.

Horsforthmariner: The idea we are "building" is absurd. Do you know what the number of first-team regulars we actually own who are under the age of 30 is? The answer is just 4 - Macca, Mills, Summerfield and Dembele (maybe 5 if you include Berrett). Of these only Dembele has a contract past next summer. We've got a squad of old-timers looking for one last payday and people who know they will be out of here come May.

We have two talented youngsters - Clifton who nearly never gets in the squad and Wright, who is upset that Town never seem to bother watching him play for a tin pot outfit. So, it can't be said that Slade is investing in our youth.

Slade can't be said to be clearing out the dross - the only players who have left are Clements, Osborne and Jones - our three most creative and talented midfielders. We're still left with the likes of Asante and McAllister who for whatever reason have been clearly frozen out. Our squad isn't smaller than when Bignot arrived. Now we just have a squad of less talented and less caring players.

Is building bringing in 30 somethings like Woolford, Dixon and Clarke(who is admittedly ok) and non-entities like Cardwell, Kelly and Hooper at the expense of club legends like Pearson and Disley, who bled for Town?

So how are we building for the future? We're not investing in our youth, were not reducing the squad and we've not bought in quality.

The reality is that this club isn't building for next season we are on the slippery slope out of this league!

Messages flooded in directed at the board.

Bigdavemariner. Morning everyone. This past 12 months or so have been a painful experience supporting Town. I've always tried to stay positive and upbeat and always tried to stick with the manager etc. however, this last couple of weeks, the embarrassing statements from the board and the complete lack of ambition shown by the club with bringing in shite players and releasing our most talented, as well as the poor standard on the pitch each week has been demoralizing.

However, the one thing that hurts the most, and I really hope that someone from the club reads this or can pass this on to John Fenty and the powers that be....

My 9-year-old lad, he was obsessed with this club. He saved his pocket money to buy shirts and bits from the club shop, we'd have fixtures written on the calendar at home planning them in (proper Dad and lad time), and we planned in away games. He would literally talk about Town non-stop and loved supporting them. I saw that passion and excitement in him as a 9-year-old that I remember myself having. As a Dad it was brilliant and lovely to see.

I think you can tell where this is going...but my 9-year-old lad has now lost all motivation, drive and passion associated with supporting Town. His favourite players that he had a connection with have gone. The likes of Shaun Pearson and Disley who generated an excitement in the team and more importantly the local community have left and taken that spirit with them. They're journeymen brought in who don't care have damaged that spirit and passion and the clowns in charge from Slade through to the board are responsible. My 9-year-old lad recognises this. 9 years old!!! He woke up this morning asking if Slade had been sacked and who we'd sold.

He has a bitterness towards supporting this club already and lost that excitement of being a Town fan. At 9 years old this is unacceptable and this poisonous atmosphere and feeling around the club is driving people away. The club have lost out of £40 a game with us both hardly ever attending because neither of us can face another miserable afternoon at Blundell Park. We live around the corner from Bradley and are actually thinking of watching Clee Town or Grimsby Borough so that we can start enjoying watching football again.

I really hope someone reads this and the management and board are aware of how the fans are feeling. I know we can't be the only ones feeling like this, but this is the sorry direction the club is heading. Sorry for the rant, but I'm bloody fed up!

Town started February with a point at home to Cheltenham

---

ginnywings: Sorry peeps but Slade is taking us down. He is using the tried and tested Neil Woods method of drawing our way to relegation.

I have seen some shit in my time but that is the worst, most unbalanced squad I have ever seen. Two young inexperienced strikers with barely a handful of games between them playing in midfield. Backed up by the most ineffective duo you could imagine, who are used to relegation. Losing our best defender and having to replace him with a midget right back against a giant front line because we have no-one else. We then have to put in a right back who is making his debut, but to be fair, he looked ok. Only one player on the pitch that is contracted for next season. Loanees everywhere you look. I just cannot see where the goals are going to come from and if you can't score goals, you can't win games.

We were pushed back for almost the entire second half and they won just about every header, loose ball and second ball going. Our answer was the usual sit back and panic, by booting the ball as high and as far as we could, only to see it come straight back again. It just looks all too familiar.

Jackson scored, then didn't do much else. Matt is about as elegant as a newborn giraffe, though he tries hard. Malik looked quick and tricky, but we were mainly out-battled by their land of the giant's players.

One thing I know, is that if you keep changing personnel and formation, grasping for a win, it usually doesn't go well. That side today bore no relation to a professionally put together and drilled football team. It all smacks of hit and hope.

Slade out.

Even the Supporters Trust wanted to sack Slade but were unable to

---

Bax: *The Mariners Trust is well aware of the groundswell of discontent around the recent run of form and the management of Russell Slade and Paul Wilkinson. This sentiment is shared by the majority of fans and members we have spoken to, and indeed the Trust Board.*

The Mariners Trust Rep Jon Wood was at the Board Meeting yesterday. After a discussion with me we formed the view that we should represent the views of the fans and Jon articulated their concerns to the rest of the board in the strongest possible terms.

Despite this, after a long debate and taking into account all factors, the rest of the board reached the outcome as detailed in the club's statement.

We now move on, respect the decision, and will do everything possible to help turn around the rest of the season.

With another four or five wins required to guarantee safety, we would urge supporters to get behind the players on the pitch and do their bit to ensure we remain in League 2 for next season.

WEEK 40

Town lost another game they needed to win when they were emphatically crushed 3-0 by Crawley away.

---

pontoonlew: *In the pub by the ground. We were on top for the first 15 minutes then it was downhill all the way.*

Just a team lacking in any direction and ideas, I'm not blaming the players and there is commitment, it's Slade and Slade alone. He has to go, it isn't a case of who to replace him, it's just him!!

I don't care if it's Buckley, Moore or Theresa May, he's clearly lost the players and just going through the motions, please Fenty act now before it's too late

---

The calls to sack Slade, if anything, had moved up another notch and were coming from all quarters now.

Hagrid: *John, I know you will read this. Please sack the management team John. You're a supporter too, you know in your heart we are heading for oblivion again. Fall on your sword and do the right thing. They must go, we cannot go on like this. The club WILL die if we go out the league again. This could be the biggest few months in our club's history because I can promise you the fans won't stand by you and the club again. I'm begging you, please sack them, for the sake of the fans, the club and the town .*

Jonnyboy82: *JUST FUCKING DO IT NOW TONIGHT I DON'T CARE HOW OR WHERE. YOU DO IT JOHN, JUST SACK HIM!!!*

Town were 17th but many now started to see relegation as an inevitability

---

scott_gtfc_89: *After today I honestly can't see us staying up but I hate to say it.*

Most the other teams below us have games in hand, some two games. I can't see us scoring never mind winning. Am at the lowest I've been with the club and I don't see a way out now even if we sacked Slade. We could be starting next season with just 4 players on the books.

What a nightmare situation. I am not angry anymore, I am just disappointed and upset the club has been let go get like this, 7 strikers on the books and we can't score, creative midfielders gone and not replaced. We even let our top goal scorer go who's not even a full striker when we can't score.

How have we got to this, after what the supporters did on Operation Promotion, getting us out the league? Please John, sack Slade, it's the ONLY THING that gives us the slightest chance of staying up.

TO HELL AND BACK

It's just broken from top to bottom.

BP Vicar took an honest stock of the squad.

BP Vicar:

Keepers: James McKeown is injured, he's needed replacing anyway since we came up. Killip is improving to be fair, it's a lot on his shoulders mind. Kean hadn't impressed before his injury.

Right backs: Mills is decent, no more than that. Davis is a great pro, a truly brilliant pro and I see him training like a loon in the gym when I go. He's probably been cardio training with the team in the morning, but he's a central midfielder who can't get around anymore. Still he's the first name on the team sheet for me and captain over Clarke.

Left Back: The only left-back Dixon is shite. I won't mess about here. A squad of 34 pros and only one left back.

Centre Backs: The ageing skipper Clarke is worse than the great Pearson we brilliantly released as he was coming to his prime. I believe they are building a statue of him in Wrexham already. Osborne is carrying a bit of weight, he seems more interested in fighting with teammates and constantly bowing to his prophet than defending. Collins showing real signs of ageing, off the ball in particular, in my opinion.

Centre midfield: Mr Invisible Berrett, Mr improved a lot, but still not scored any goals despite a million shots on goal and gives the ball away. Summerfield, Rose who is good and shite in the same game, he says asthma isn't a problem, he will as it's his living so why so up and down in the same game? Clifton must be shocking to be kept out of the team by these clowns.

Left midfield: Real toughie here, we have Woolford who has his slippers on and seeing his days out, Wilks who looks our best player since signing but keeps getting taken off (and he's a striker apparently).

Right Midfield: The right wing is Dembele who was brilliant up to about ten weeks ago but is apparently injured, then plays, badly, then is injured the next game. What's going on there?

Forwards: Matt is a clumsy donkey who shows the ball on his right foot all the time, doesn't bother shielding it. Vernon is looking his age, we have loan players like Jackson who is clearly on his way down but could be the saviour, Verman or something like that (I lose track of the *names), who is a clever player. Can Verman and Jackson play together given their size? I don't see how. Plenty of other strikers to mention, I haven't that long.*

I've missed a few, possibly unfair, possibly I've had enough. But I look at this squad of misfits, apparently there is a good team spirit and the dressing room is jovial and they are all in it together. I doubt most of them know their 'mates' names as I have proper lost track.

Great management Russ, you've got rid of all the players with some ability, brought in ageing journeyman and young lads on loan with no ties to the club. You have done particularly well to get rid of any creativity we had, good luck on being a 'builder' when most players apart from the proper shit ones are out of contract or over 35. Slade could not have done a worse job of dismantling a side if he tried. It's so inept it is beyond belief.

We've seen this before, and we know how it goes. Slade has to go, Fenty has to go.

Two days after the Crawley game Slade was sacked by Grimsby on 11 February 2018 after seeing the team fail to win in 12 league games, with eight losses, he left the team 17th in League Two. It was treated with jubilation.

EY Mariner: *I take no pleasure in the announcement this afternoon.*
I never wanted Russell Slade back in our dugout in the first place, but I still wanted things to work out better than what they did. However, it's clear to me that the main person he has to blame for his departure is himself. When he came in, he had a promising group of players to work with. It was a group who, with the right additions in the right areas of the field, could have challenged at the right end of the table this season. Instead, he tried to fix something which was nowhere near as broken as the level of change we have seen suggested and I'm afraid he, but more so we, have paid for that.

MarinerRob: *Fantastic! Back to Blundell Park next Saturday. VERY happy.*

Mariner Ronnie: *You'll be on your own!*

A few half-hearted suggestions were heard for Paul Wilkinson to be given the job, but he effectively got first chance as he became caretaker, with nobody yet lined up as a permanent replacement.

Pontoonlew: Personally, I don't want anybody who has had any part in this sham of a few months being made the next manager.

That said, he will have my full support until a new manager comes in or he somehow proves he can take the club forward.

sam gy: People are annoyed about Wilko being in temporary charge; maybe just stop moaning for a bit and get behind the man. Slade has gone.

Also, stop pretending that you have any idea about how his working relationship was with Slade and how much input he had. You don't know.

Yes, he has been the ASSISTANT to a very unsuccessful manager, but he's still had a great coaching career and is better placed than Dave Moore to take temporary charge.

WEEK 41

The sad news that long-time Town writer Steve Plowes had passed away was greeted with some fond memories.

Barralad: I've just heard the very sad news that Steve Plowes one of the original contributors to "Sing When We're Fishing" has passed away.

Steve was a great Town fan long exiled to the Blackpool coast blessed with a brilliant sense of (often gallows) humour.

R.I.P. Steve.

Link to more memories: https://forum.thefishy.co.uk/Blah.pl?m-1518550483/

Town followed the drubbing at Crawley with another loss at Cambridge, in which 'keeper James McKeown finally returned for the first time since Boxing Day. Whatever

Wilkinson was doing it was not working, but was the fundamental problem the players Grimsby had?

Vernon angered Town fans by making a gesture at them as he was warming up (for which he subsequently apologised).

Freemoash88: That's right ladies and gentlemen it's all over social media and being discussed on Radio Humberside, Scott Vernon giving Town fans the wanker sign at the end of the game and pathetic Kelly also laughing at the sad gesture.

This is becoming a joke. Please Fenty get rid of these two clowns, the biggest wage stealers since the days of Adam Proudlock and co.

ginnywings: We had 5 players on the pitch today that came from relegated sides. The York duo were part of a side that got the lowest points total I can ever remember. Clarke from relegated Coventry. Hooper and Kelly from Port Vale. Not to mention 4 loanees at various stages of the game. When the management is bringing in such winners, sanctioned by the board, you can see why we are in the mess we are.

If that wasn't bad enough, we have had three managers and two caretaker managers in less than 2 seasons. We are about to employ our 4th.

If you set out to purposefully destroy a promoted team, you couldn't have done a better job of it.

The hunt for a successor saw many of the managers Town fans would like to see ruled out, because Grimsby at this moment in their history were not that big a draw. Town were going to have pick someone who was either once good, but fallen on hard times (like Slade), or alternatively someone unproven at this level who just might make it (like Bignot or Hurst).

Hagrid: You have to ask yourself - and I hate saying this - why would either come here? At this moment in time Lincoln are bigger than us, have huge crowds and they have Wembley coming up. It just won't happen

Shilts: Of all names mentioned already my vote goes to Craig Elliot at Boston. I am sick of journeyman players and managers on the merry go round. Why get a bigger name manager *that had success once with a club in League One but has since been hired and fired from 5 different jobs in the last 10yrs?*

Instead get a winner from leagues below (Lincoln should know that), and all our previous best came as winners from below, Buckley and Hurst were nobodies till they came here (when I say nobodies, I mean managers on the up with proven records, but as yet unknown to us)

There's plenty out there that know only success and promotion, a la Cowleys.

It would be a rapid rise for Elliot, he was managing Shaw Lane a season ago!!!

But he won 3 promotions with them in 4 seasons and left for Boston when they were 3pts off top with games in hand.

Now he's completely turned Boston round from a situation just like ours currently. I want a bit of that.

Someone used to a budget as well and knows the lower leagues.

Not another Slade type.

If Fenty can't get an appointment right or do the relevant checks, clearly the Boston chairman can, and has an eye for a manager (Hurst, now Elliot), so if we poach their managers you know that the manager has been vetted by a competent chairman also.

Wilkinson had all but ruled himself out, with the games under him so far resembling a complete continuation of the Russell Slade era.

1mickylyons: *I wanted to believe in Wilko like I believed in him as a player he always gave 100% for the shirt. As soon as I saw his team selection my heart sank the usual wasters in the matchday squad Clifton and the Villa kid should have been a brave new dawn. The 90 mins against Cambridge should be his last involvement from the dugout the bravery he showed as a player clearly hasn't moved across into coaching/management. The interview full of buzzwords and BS about hard work. You don't need to work harder Paul you need to do the right work and that means leaving out the matchday squad the likes of Vernon, Kelly, Dixon and Hooper who are 4 of the worst players most of us have ever seen. You let us down Paul and worse still you let yourself down had you got a result yesterday with kids BP would have had 5k on Saturday all backing you to the hilt. No backbone, no desire, no hope and little effort :-/*

The Old Codger. Messrs Fenty, Day, Marley & Chapman. You'd best get your chequebook and your prayer mats out because this shower of shite (manager & players) will cost you any shred of credibility you still retain as the board who, not once, but twice condemned our proud club to the non-league.

John Fenty explained in an interview the reason for sacking Slade, the timing and the hunt for a "hungry young manager".

Mariner_09. He said:

- it was a difficult decision.
- that hard work is all well and good but sometimes it isn't enough.
- we haven't had "lady luck" in recent weeks and that the penalty decision was questionable on Saturday.
- Slade cannot say that the board haven't given him time to turn things around but the form has been too poor. He added that fans want "knee-jerk reactions" and the board has to "hold its cool".
- They've had a whole raft of applications, they're going through them and, interestingly, will proceed to making approaches for permission to speak to candidates.
- said he didn't reveal the length of contract because sections of the media "ridiculed" a 6-month rolling contract suggesting it didn't give suitable protection.
- he said it works for the club and he's had nightmares with managers on 3-year contracts and he has never known a manager turn down an appointment because of a rolling contract.
- he said the atmosphere against Cheltenham was better, the Fenty out stuff was channelled in the right manner it and needed to be maintained so results would improve.

Cambs Mariner. Good post. Lincoln are in the fortunate position, for now, of having a owner who is willing and able to put money into the club. He also recognised the potential of the Cowley brothers but to be fair to the GTFC board they also recognised the potential of Scott and Hurst. Even though that partnership didn't work out they did persevere with Hurst and he did get us back into League Two. The big difference between the clubs then became obvious. Lincoln gave the Cowley brothers a long contract and money to spend on decent players. The board of Grimsby Town wouldn't give Hurst a better contract, or more money to bring in decent players.

pen penfras (in reply): So what the club should have done is given Hurst a 5-year contract despite a fairly large portion of the fans trying to drive him out for the last few years of his tenure. Can you imagine the uproar if that had happened? It's all well and good in hindsight saying that Hurst was brilliant, but it was only after he got us promoted that he got a bit of a break and by that time the damage was already done. And it's only after the job he's done at Shrewsbury that people have overwhelmingly decided he is a good manager.

And apparently, we should have spent more money, which would mean increasing the benign loans that everybody is so against. You can't moan at a lack of 'investment' on one hand and then moan that benign loans hold the club back on the other.

Fenty + co were faced with a difficult job to pick the right man and go some way to placating the fans.

Cambs Mariner: The club is a shambles from top to bottom. Thanks J S Fenty and the rest of the non-entities on the board.

You took us into the non-league in 2010. We got back into the League in 2016 thanks to Operation Promotion.

This season the club have dropped down to levels of incompetence, on and off the field, that I have never experienced in 48 years of watching football.

I blame you John Sheldon Fenty. It is your fault the club are where they are.

The way this season has gone I couldn't give 2 monkey's fucks if you and the rest of the board left tomorrow.

We won't and shouldn't be held to ransom by you and your ego just because you were in the fortunate position of having money.

You have cost the club more in the crap decisions you have made.

The heartache you have given to the fans far outweighs anything you have invested into the club.

WEEK 42

Grimsby's disastrous run continued with another home defeat, this time to Exeter City. The day proved to be a nightmare scenario for Town as 4 of the other 5 teams in the bottom 6 all won, and the Mariners are undeniably now part of the relegation battle. It was a game changer.

Town were given every opportunity to get at least a point as Exeter barely created a chance all game. Their only opportunity came from a Jayden Stockley penalty, but the ref awarded Grimsby a spot-kick from which Hooper completely missed the goal.

Sonofmadeleymariner: *Just back to the car. Much better. The players looked confident, aggressive and willing to attack. The peno looked soft from where I was but probably a peno. Hooper once again proved why he shouldn't be on the pitch and we couldn't hit the broad side of a barn with a shotgun from two feet away.*

However, we were better. Clifton looked good, he looked sharp, committed and confident very good full debut (why wasn't he being played?). Mills looked a real leader today commanding Clifton, guiding him, telling him where to go whilst still being on point for his defensive and attacking duties. Dixon probably had his best game today. DJ was impressive and looked a more rounded player today.

ginnywings: *It was getting toward the last knockings of the game. Frustration was building as usual, when my nephew got his phone out and looked at the other scores. He suddenly stood up and shouted over to the area the board occupy "we are going down, have you seen the other scores?", to which JF shouted back an obscenity. My nephew then shouted one back. Of course, the stewards came straight over to us, as it seems it's ok for the majority shareholder to swear in front of women and kids, but not us. I pointed out that JF swore at us first and he mumbles something about everyone being upset, then wandered back over to his guard duty of protecting the front of the area where the directors sit. I should have chinned him and got myself a 5-year ban to save myself from having to watch any more of that shite. I haven't seen a win since November and only 2 goals in 2018, and they wonder why they get stick.*

Do you know what John, you don't get to tell us when we can and when we can't complain, and you don't get to tell us where we can do it either. I wish you would now just leave the club and put us into admin if you have to. I'd rather watch a reformed GTFC at King George stadium than watch you lot on the board continue to destroy this club. It's painful. There is not one ounce of joy left in being a GTFC fan, so thank you all for that.

Macclesfield boss John Askey became the strong favourite for the job, prompting Macc fans to come on the Fishy and thank him.

Maccfan I have been reading about this all day and had to comment. If John [Askey] does leave us for you (praying to the football gods he stays) then you'll have a cracking manager. He's put together an unbelievable team this year from scratch with no budget and no backing from our useless owners. I hope your reliable source is Big Dave from the pub who heard about it of his mate Jeff.

Some fans were despondent that whoever the new boss was he should be at least given a chance by the fans.

TAGG: Yes another great decision by Fenty. Two days before Slade was appointed I posted on here 'SLADE OUT' and got the same shit as I am now. That's why The Fishy is so great!

sam gy (in reply): Yes, you are a genius. Jesus, forgive me for I have sinned. I didn't want our new manager sacked instantly, and I was prepared to give him my backing because...you know....I support my football club.

I know the club gives us very little to hang on to when it comes to supporting the club, but if we can't even have a tiny sense of optimism that a manager might do ok, then really....what's the fucking point?

It's time to shut up.

To the board - the genuine fans do not need pleading with to back the players.

To the fans who boo and insult the players - you are not doing the club any favours. If you are a real fan, get behind the players and help then retain League status. If you want to protest, do it after the final whistle or stay away.

To the players - keep calm and do your best.

Civvy at last: Whoever the new manager may be, they will have my full support until they give me reason not to give it.

Whoever we get, it will please some, and disappoint others. That's the nature of the beast.

I wasn't going to go on Saturday, but with a new manager I will be. I will also be behind the players as well and that includes Vernon.

I'm not happy with our squad, far from it. But booing anyone from the start will not achieve a thing.

It's not easy to move on, but I'm trying. We sometimes blame the players for their lack of commitment. Let's not be guilty of the same offence.

Biccys: *I'm no Fenty fan but this isn't news to him. He wants out but also as a fan he doesn't want to throw the baby out with the bath water and allow the club to die on its arse. While it's easy for anyone to say "walk away John!" He has his loans hanging around the club's neck. He's effectively holding you and me to ransom with them. I'm not part of the established football elite so don't know if this situation is standard or not. I suspect it's not though or we'd hear many tales of such events. Ask John if he's prepared to write them off and he asks why should he? Can anyone answer that honestly? My response would be that because he's expecting to have all the benefits of being a football club Chairman without spending a bean. His "friendly" (quote) loans aren't friendly at all. They're poisonous to anyone looking to take on the club. The absolute antithesis of friendly.*

There are major shareholders of many companies that have lost far more than £2m in what, 12 years? It's baffling how his thinking works. Yes, he got us out of the tax shit hole. Thanks fella, well done. So now, 10 years later we get to accept 6 years of non-league, awful football, awful players and shit facilities and impending doom again? Errrrrr, no. Not again thanks. Walk away and I guarantee there will be others far better at running a football club then you waiting to pick up the reins.

JF put his head above the parapet and received predictable criticism. With some fans criticising the board for being quiet, others were annoyed with the fact that the board were communicating at all!

Darren9: *Some points I've noticed:*

Firstly. The statement issued yesterday ended "We will not be making any further comment at this time".

If only that were true. There was no need to make this statement. If it were to cover the Scott Vernon incident then a simple release saying they've looked into it and due to extreme provocation the club will not be taking any action and that the gesture was not aimed at the fans as an entirety but at a specific individual who was targeting the player.

I have been subjected to personal abuse due to my job and I agree that it is deplorable and fully understand why Vernon made the gesture. I think we should move on from it now and put it to bed. But this is my personal opinion

The rest of the video is waffle of the highest order. Of course, he doesn't want protests. They're protesting against him and his mates. He's going to "plea" against, isn't he? But does he really think that this is going to solve the issue? If anything, I'd suggest that it is just going to make it worse. Inside or outside BP or any other ground doesn't matter, does it? We've backed the club and the players we have and look where it's got us. Can he really, truly expect that we'll be clapping them for every shite touch, misplaced pass and bottled challenge? In any case we're not protesting against them as individuals but complaining against the situation were in. I think that is understandable.

On the subject of a new manager. Well I maintain my stance that he's hoping for some "footballing fortune" in the form of a fluked win so he can appoint Wilkinson either until the end of the season on one of those lovely 6-month rolling contracts.

I said earlier and I'll say again there was no need to do this video.

Who is JF anyway? He's not the chairman, is he? If there is a statement it should come from the chairman. He wants all the power of chairman but spat his dummy out about being one long ago.

A dignified silence on all matters would have been better than this video which has done nothing but further antagonise the section of fans he was hoping to appease and to further stoke his massive ego.

As well as a new manager, team, ground, training facilities and owners, the one thing this club needs is a fully functioning PR department who could tell him what a bad idea this was.

As for the actual video. Well, it was poorly framed, badly lit and those making it couldn't be bothered to turn their phones off.

On a plus point JF's shawl neck sweater was nicer than his roll neck/leather jacket combo at the fans' forum so at least he can't be pilloried for that and we're moving forward in the building in that regard.

RoboCod: *Pity he and the board don't listen to the fans' pleas. When they pleaded, almost to a man/woman to change things before Xmas, to stop the most rotten of all rots with Slade's hapless management which was not going to improve.*

Instead we got...a statement. A statement backing Slade, suggesting we stick together and the corner would be turned.

Now we look for a new man with a horribly unbalanced squad who have got into a losing habit, with the transfer window shut and a bunch of loanees who will be gone in a puff of dust come the final day, with a level of distrust between fans and board on a level I've never seen before.

I doubt we'll see anyone of any worth come in to manage, but it wouldn't be beyond this bunch of clowns to take Wilko on as a result of little interest in the job and pretend he was top choice anyway. I expect this now, sadly.

WEEK 43

The news that Wilko would be staying (as assistant) was greeted with dismay.

Bigdog: *Forcing an assistant manager on prospective managerial candidates would be penny-pinching, thoroughly unprofessional, stupid and short-sighted, especially if it's a sticking point in negotiations with the best candidates. The relationship between a manager and his assistant is a highly personal one. Every manager at a well-run professional football club should be able to pick his own backroom staff.*

Mighty_Mariner: *One of the most important appointments in our history is what Fenty said! Waiting for the right man, looking for your up and coming managers I get that. But far more importantly is whoever the best candidate is, for god's sake give them the tools they require to be able to do the job properly. INCLUDING choosing their own backroom staff! The success of most managers lies heavily with who they've got backing them up. Look at Brian Clough, Sir Alex Ferguson etc etc... They've always had very very good assistant managers alongside them.*

FFS Fenty, choose the best candidate available and let him choose who they want to bring in, don't force an assistant manager on them and let that be a reason to turn us down.

Is it really that fucking difficult!!!

Swansea Mariner: *It's totally ridiculous the manager should pick their own backroom staff. How come we get everything arse end round. Total joke of a club.*

The inevitable cries for Buckley had few supporters

---

ginnywings: *Easy as that. Drag a bloke out of retirement and within a week we will be passing the ball around like Brazil. Just leave him to his co-commentating and enjoy the memories.*

With fans now seriously expecting relegation, everyone was wondering if they would keep going if Town went down.

1mickylyons: *Not for me it's unthinkable the same bloke could let this happen twice in such a short space of time if we go down I won't return until he has gone sadly.*

BP Vicar: *I won't be going anymore. The club have used up all of my good will and really are taking the piss now with these levels of ineptitude.*

With Askey out the way, Gary Holt was the next name in the frame.

---

ginnywings: *Nobody knows really do they? Holt could do a great job or be a disaster. The same with Wilko, the same with anyone you care to mention. Bellamy could be a great shout, or he could be the next Tony Adams or Paul Merson. Every manager is a gamble. Some click, some don't. You can do your due diligence and get Paul Hurst who was about 4th or 5th choice, or you could get Marcus Bignot, who was the "outstanding candidate".*

I'm just praying that whoever they choose, he does the business, because the club is dying on its arse.

GrimRob: *Holt has done nothing for two years. "Holt left Norwich by mutual consent after the 201-16 season"*

His career has holted ;)

Definite no for me, I'd prefer Jolley of the names bandied about

---

Nobody really wanted Holt, but there was starting to be one person who the fans overwhelmingly backed in all the polls. Few had heard of the new favourite when Slade was sacked, but he came over well in his YouTube videos. His name was Michael Jolley.

MarinerMal: *He sounds like the ideal candidate but I doubt he'll manage GTFC.*

He's intelligent, articulate and with a Cambridge education. He's not shy of expressing his opinion or disagreeing with the board.

Fenty would feel intimidated and would be afraid of losing control. There is no way he'll put someone in charge like that. He wants a 'yes' man.

Sweden: *Give him a contract and let him remain whatever happens this year. Show a little long-term perspective and focus on local younger abilities. I think that in Sweden we are better off seeing it in the long term.*

Bigdog: *I try not to call out for one manager or another as there are so many variables we don't know about at this level. We know bits and bobs about their public persona, for the young and upcoming there's very little in the way of managerial records to go on, we don't know what's on the table to them as a financial package, playing budget or management infrastructure and we know very little about their personal character not being privy to the interview process. We can all go on what we can find online and go with our gut instinct. I've got no qualms against anyone nailing their colours to the mast of any candidate as I'm none the wiser myself. I've got ideas regarding the right profile and also fears about JF keeping within his own personal comfort zone as he has done in the past, but that's about it. I'll have a gut reaction to the appointment when it eventually rears its head like everyone else, then wait and see what happens over the rest of the season and beyond before making a more rounded judgement..*

What has struck me though is how low the perceived calibre of candidate is for us compared to who's in the running for the Oxford, Peterborough and Mansfield vacancies. All I know is, if this scenario happened a good fifteen years ago, we wouldn't have been the bottom feeders out of this group of clubs when looking for a manager..

Jonnyboy82: *GET JOLLEY YOU IMBECILES.*

Meanwhile applications continued to trickle in.

IlkleyMariner: *Dear Mr Non-Chairperson*
I would like to apply for the position of GTFC Manager.
I have been retired for a bit so am used to working from home and looking after children.
I don't live near Cleethorpes so am ideally placed.
I could share a lift to training and save on travel expenses.
I once played against Radcliffe Borough Reserves and scored a consolation goal, so have lots of potential
I can't make an interview at the moment as I am snowed in, but I know that you are not in a rush to appoint so can come over when the weather gets warmer.
Please let me know when you want to see me.

PS I saw Paul Wilkinson score at Everton, so I like him.

The table was starting to see Town's position look increasingly perilous, and they seemed to be relying on the bottom two losing, more than escaping trouble through their own success. It was hard to imagine many points coming Grimsby's way after 14 games without a win. On the plus side, the Mariners still had to play the bottom three at Blundell Park. If they won them all, that might be enough, but it looked a huge ask, with such a poor, out of form side.

Pos	Team	P	W	D	L	F	A	GD	Pts
1	Luton	34	20	8	6	74	34	+40	68
2	Accrington	34	20	5	9	58	38	+20	65
3	Wycombe	35	18	8	9	67	51	+16	62
4	Notts County	35	17	10	8	56	36	+20	61
5	Mansfield	34	16	12	6	53	35	+18	60
6	Exeter	33	18	4	11	44	37	+7	58
7	Swindon	35	18	3	14	55	51	+4	57
8	Coventry	34	16	6	12	38	28	+10	54
9	Lincoln	34	14	11	9	46	37	+9	53
10	Carlisle	35	14	9	12	50	45	+5	51
11	Crawley Town	35	15	6	14	41	43	-2	51
12	Colchester	35	13	11	11	45	41	+4	50
13	Newport County	34	12	12	10	41	43	-2	48
14	Cambridge	35	13	9	13	35	45	-10	48
15	Stevenage	35	11	9	15	46	51	-5	42
16	Cheltenham	35	10	10	15	48	52	-4	40
17	Yeovil	34	10	8	16	46	55	-9	38
18	Crewe	35	11	3	21	41	57	-16	36
19	Forest Green	34	10	6	18	39	56	-17	36
20	Grimsby	35	9	9	17	30	51	-21	36
21	Morecambe	33	8	11	14	34	44	-10	35
22	Port Vale	34	9	8	17	37	49	-12	35
23	Chesterfield	34	8	6	20	35	61	-26	30
24	Barnet	35	7	8	20	33	52	-19	29

League Table 28th February

MARCH

Pointless

WEEK 43

Michael Jolley was appointed at the start of March and the first contact he had with many fans was on Twitter, although he immediately promised to close his account.

Link: https://twitter.com/michaeljolley07/status/969641730520821763

Mighty Mariner: *They've actually listened!!! Jolley Appointed as new GTFC manager!!! I am very, very happy indeed!!*

The Old Codger: *He can take over the PR too!*

Squinter: *I am impressed with him already :-*
1) Already done his research and been to last two games
2) Moving to the area
3) Coming off Twitter.

RoboCod: *"Michael has a track record of playing an exciting, high-pressing, attacking style of football. Michael will create a tactically astute, cohesive group with a focus on an ethos of youth development at the heart of his philosophy."*

My heart is all a flutter. Please, please let this one work out.

After all the criticism, the anger directed at the board dissipated a bit as a realisation that Town had given themselves a chance surfaced.

Mariner93er: *Credit to the board. It's as simple as that really. Despite a lot of criticism from me included, they've made an exciting appointment and have surely brought the fans together. The statement was also a very positive one, and if we stay up, we could be dragging ourselves in the right direction. Still a long way to go this season, but a step in the right direction.*

With 10 games left, posters begin to think about what Town needed to do to turn this around: things like supporting the team, backing the players, and basically becoming fans again.

Mrs Doyle: *Right Fenty time to get your brain in gear. From now until the season's end at home half price entrance. Give the Osmond end to Town fans put the away fans in compost corner.*

Offer existing season ticket holders a discount for next season.

We need to give Mike Jolley and the team the twelfth man, pack the park and sing our hearts out.

Jolley has got a massive task, we need to close ranks and help him.

It was time to stop the criticism and back the side in the final few crucial games.

TheRonRaffertyFanClub: *This is not helping anyone. These are professional footballers not fools or con merchants like some we have had, and they know the side is failing. They don't need this sort of extra moanalot exhortation pressure when the name of the game is to get the goal that will set us on the right track.*

Poojah was right for that time. It is not right for now. We have a new manager, players need to impress, they will try to impress. That is human nature. Help them to do it, don't hammer them further into the turf than they already are.

Wilkinson's final act was to pick the team at Carlisle. Town inevitably lost as Jolley watched from the stand.

Mikey_345: *I am starting to wish he went with Slade. Today's team selection was an absolute fucking disgrace!*

How the hell are we meant to score, let alone win a game with 2 relatively immobile forwards and three of the most uncreative centre midfielders I've ever seen.

Zero pace, zero creativity (until Vernam came on far too late) and zero passion.

The scary thing is teams don't have to get out of second gear to beat us at the minute.

WEEK 44

For once fans were looking forward to a game at BP rather than trudging along in hope and because they had a season ticket.

Badger57: *I've got my GTFC mojo back! I can't wait for the game tomorrow and am genuinely excited for the first time in ages!*

Yeah, I know, I know. I'm just setting myself up for more misery and disappointment. It's the same players blah blah blah.... BUT maybe, just maybe a new brighter dawn is breaking? :D

The Dogs Testicles: *It would be great to hear a return of the FISH chant for Saturday!!*

Can you all recall Wembley, it was deafening and then when we played Morecambe in our first game back in the Football League? The players walked out to that amazing sound that must have sent goosebumps up the back of their necks!!

It's never too late, let's do this!! All Town aren't we??!!

Drums will be there and this is definitely the chant that should greet MJ and the team for Saturday!!!

Time to Unite, WE ARE TOWN!!!

Grimsby salvaged a point with a late equaliser against Port Vale. Defeat would have been a disaster, but a point was not really good enough either. Still, it at least felt a little better, even if the game had been marred by 1980s-style fighting which had caused a lengthy stop in play.

Goalkeeper James McKeown (Macca) won praise for his part in the game.

Mikey_345: *Think the lad [Macca] deserves a thread of his own tonight. He was outstanding today, and single-handedly kept us in that.*

Skrill: *I don't care what people say, Macca's a Grimsby legend.*

Grimps: *I'm not being funny but you don't have to have an NVQ in safety at football matches or whatever worthless qualification or safety officer has to know that if there is likely to be trouble at Blundell Park you take the away fans out the Harrington street side of the ground .*

Also when did a couple of parked minibuses became the segregation between the home and away fans ?

This idiot is great at making 13-year-olds sit down in the Pontoon but has no idea when it comes to performing his real job

heppy8: *Unfortunately, for those taking part the buzz of the fight is more important than what's happening on the pitch, more important than their team maintaining momentum. It's so obviously more important than staying in the league. I hated it in the eighties and the nineties and now it just makes me sad that blokes in their forties and fifties feel the need to act like apes. They must lead sad lives and have tiny cocks.*

Mariner91: *I can't help but take issue with that comment. I lead a sad life and have a tiny cock but I've never behaved like that.*

TO HELL AND BACK

The match with Port Vale was marred by crowd trouble following Grimsby's late equaliser when sections of the two sets of fans clashed, causing a lengthy stoppage.

Adam0202: *Hello lads and lasses, Vale fan here, I just thought I'd offer my thoughts if you don't object. I was there having driven up with my lad and parked by Sidney Park. Can I quell any misinformation about Stoke lads being with Vale, it has not and would never ever happen so sorry to whoever posted but that it is drivel.*

At our home game in October the Police Intelligence estimated 1200 GTFC fans and a potential for disorder. The reason I know this is because one of the lads who usually comes with us is Plod.

Anyone who came to that game would of thought the Queen or Theresa May was at the game, I have never seen so many old bill in my life. Total overkill but given Saturday's events maybe not. I think you bought about 600-ish if my memory serves me right.

*On to events on Saturday, I am a 48-year-old bloke who has followed Vale home and away for years. It was **well** known down here that there were 2 bus loads of so-called 'lads' going to the game. No idea what went wrong between Staffs' plod and is it Humberside plod?*

We have attracted an albeit younger chavvy mob of clowns over the past couple of seasons. The games they usually attend would be the likes of Bolton and Sheff Utd where there was quite serious trouble last season.

This season the games they were targeting were Lincoln, Grimsby and Mansfield. Lincoln was a damp squib because about 40 of them went to Benidorm on a Stag do.

Saturday was well known about and based also on the reputation yourselves have. The same clowns will be at Mansfield in about a month's time.

Clearly the goal was the spark for the violence but I believe they had made themselves known in Cleethorpes before the game.

After the game me and my lad pretty much kept our gobs shut as it wasn't a nice experience walking back to the car.

Neither set of fans covered themselves in glory, though our idiots clearly started the trouble.

I felt sorry for the stewards who were literally on a hiding to nothing. My overall moan has to be with the old bill, if someone like me knew that there were 2 bus loads going up then what on earth were they doing/thinking?

I have seen moans about your chairmen etc not wanting to pay the costs so I can't comment on that.

Petty maybe this bit but the bloke who did the aerial video sounded an absolute moron too, some of his comments were bizarre.

Let us hope that this doesn't start some sort of idiotic tit for tat rivalry between us because if we both manage to stay up I can imagine some sort of revenge mission would be on the cards next season.

It was a great atmosphere too in our end spoilt by the antics of a minority.
Whilst I am no angel and can handle myself I can honestly say I have never been to a football game with the intention of kicking someone's head in.

Good luck in staying up as you are a proper club and hope you don't mind my observations.

There were at least signs of an improvement despite Town not getting three points, and still 16 games without a win. The fans were beginning to realise that their support was key, and they had to back the players they had as nobody else was going to get them out of this mess.

The Old Codger: *Can everyone please keep their thoughts about individual players to themselves until after the final whistle? MJ has been given a 10-game window to save us from the abyss that is the National League and, to a man/woman/child, we need to be behind all 11 that go on the pitch.*

Tommy *(replying to someone asking who should be allowed to leave in the summer): This sort of thing might as well be left until the end of the season now IMO.*

Doesn't help when some of those you suggest paying off immediately might be guys we're relying on to perform and keep us up. And we also don't know how everyone will react to different coaching, managing and playing styles that the new manager might employ.

WEEK 45

After Michael Jolley's first point, Town had two tough away games. The second was at Coventry, but the first was at Lincoln, a match that always stands alone in the fixture list because of the proximity of the two towns. City were having a good season and looked likely to at least make the play-offs. Town were fighting for their lives at the other end of the table. There was more than just pride at stake.

Grimsby had been relegated in 2010 and Lincoln in 2011. City though had made a better start to life in the Football League while Town could be heading back to where they came from. Many supporters were already making comparisons with the relegation side of 2010.

Bax: Because not only have we not learned a single lesson from 2010, we've made exactly the same mistakes. Exactly the same.

A bloated squad full of journeymen and loanees, a manager he should never have appointed in the first place and then sacked far too late.

We haven't so much managed to sleepwalk into relegation but been in Freefall and it's all been so utterly predictable and preventative. Instead of leading and taking action, the club is too busy policing social media and stalking the Fishy dishing out warnings for stuff they don't like. In fairness the entire board is culpable. All of them.

JF told me personally Operation Promotion was the worst thing that ever happened because of the pressure it put the club under.

That will be nothing to the pressure if he takes us down again. And there's no blaming the fans for this one John.

BP Vicar: BP Vicar's club policy list

*Release 37 goal strikers as they 'haven't scored many against top six teams'.

*Release centre back leaders coming to their prime, pillars of the community. Especially as the skipper was getting on and needed replacing.

PTO

*Do not ever negotiate contracts with players who have dedicated themselves, proved themselves and excelled. Especially when there are only a few months left of their contracts. This will allow other clubs to monitor their availability and make contact with their agents and get deals done.

*Sign players looking for their last contracts, just so they can pop their slippers on and coast through to retirement, really good if you can sign a load of defenders coming to the end of their playing career at the same time. Ideal that.

*Under no circumstances make moves early in pre-season. Wait until the very last minute so wages can be saved and the dregs nobody else wants are available. Really useful to minimise the chances of players 'gelling' and getting to know the 'style of play' lol.

*Alienate squad members by treating them like lepers, reducing morale within the squad. Especially when the lepers (Clements, McAllister) are better than the players 'ahead' of them.

*Make sure any player showing any sign of ability is moved on asap.

*Loan players out to other clubs fighting relegation - ensure no recall clause is in the agreement.

*Local media outlets are not to be allowed to draw their own conclusions or to publicise anything other than the gospel of the club. Failure to adhere to this instruction will mean player interviews are suspended. Make sure high-ranking officials (preferably wearing a roll up to the neck turtle jumper and leather jacket) make an utter arse of themselves.

Amendments / Poster additions

(Courtesy of Robocod)
* Curtail any old-fashioned excitement for fans when entering the final day of the transfer market by not only failing to bring in someone who can grab some extra goals but selling your top scorer, the only player who has scored a half decent amount all season, and relying on your current lumbering big striker who didn't want to join you in the first place but who found nothing better so joined on loan, and anyway he 'puts in a shift' every other game even though this isn't strictly true it's just that the current talentless Town team make everything look like hard work.

(Courtesy of The Old Codger)
*Bury the club in as much debt as possible in order to create a Putinesque dictatorship

(Courtesy of Quagmire)
*Make sure a significant number of signings are players who have a losing mentality, by signing players who have suffered relegation in their previous season ie Summerfield, Berrett,

Clarke, Hooper, Kelly, Rose (seconds away from relegation to the Conference last season with Newport) etc

(Courtesy of The Old Codger)
*Appoint a director that has been auditing the accounts so he knows all the sums and where they are hiding. Then enrol him on the same charisma-bypass course that all GTFC directors are obliged to attend. Once trained, pat him on the head and train him to say 'Shut up!'

Can anyone else think of any other wonderful policies we could use?

Swansea_Mariner: *WTF we are 38 games into a season and a new manager comes and has to start giving out nutrition plans. These are supposed to be professional athletes.*

I am so angry at Slade, this sort of thing beggars belief.

The new loan players were not working out, and fans were even turning on them. Michael Jolley signed Andrew Fox and Gary McSheffrey to boost Slade's squad but the win still eluded Town.

---

chaos33 *(defending Gary McSheffrey): Why don't we just treat individual players on merit and give him a few games before judging? He might turn out to be an inspired, decisive signing. How about that?*

Finally, the big match day arrived, and Town turned up in numbers, as did (for once) Lincoln.

---

moosey_club: *Reports that there are large groups of Lincoln fans searching out Grimsby fans in the city centre, they are asking for directions to Sincil Bank :)*

But the match went badly, and Town lost 3-1 to the Imps.

Civvy at last: *Fuck off John Fenty. You picked Slade. You let him get rid of our best players. You saved two quid. And I'm stood on a terrace totally embarrassed.*

I won't be there for non-league. Hopefully neither will you.

Although some blamed Jolley, most kept faith in the new Town boss (for now).

Swansea_Mariner*: I love the way people are saying he's Slade mk3 because he's not doing exactly what they want. I assume you mean picking McAllister and DJ. One player who has played a handful of games in 2 years and the other with 1 goal and 0 assists this season.*

Points of difference so far between Jolley and Slade:

1: Jolley has played Clifton;
2: Jolley has played Sullliman (Port Vale);
3: Jolley has changed tactics and formation within the same game (Port Vale);
4: Jolley has signed a second left back for the squad addressing a long-held issue on this board;
5: According to RH Jolley has issued nutritional plans to all players;
6: According to a current player (allegedly from the other thread on a troublemaker) Jolley has improved and professionalised training.

Points 1-4 have been a source of long-term moaning on this board and have been addressed. I would expect Sulliman to come back in after international duty.

As for Woolford he hasn't seen him play yet as he hasn't been in the team for a while so he's bound to want to see what he's got in a game situation. As for Berrett well who else do we have, oh yes McAllister who has hardly played in 2 years. I agree its worth a go, unless there is something majorly wrong that we don't know I would expect Jolley to try him at some point.

*We are **two** weeks in! Give the guy a chance!*

chicaneuk*: Sorry guys - turning on the manager TWO WEEKS into the job is just unfathomable.*

LH *Well, I reckon we're fucked but while we've still got a chance I'll back them. The short space of time in which we conceded the goals really killed it. What a fine job Slade and "the club" have done with recruitment this season, eh?*

Got to say Lincoln are streets ahead of us in most respects now. I hope "some people" are sitting at home wondering why Lincoln's fanbase is probably 10-20 years younger than ours as an average, why their ground is full despite achieving no more thus far than we did last season etc etc.

That said there was some odd stuff about them. Firstly the mosaic was impressive - although maybe a bit imperial Japan - but what was that banner about? You've been better than us three seasons in the last eight - the shadow is near enough non-existent. What was that hideously overweight div in front of the 617 lot doing with a Town shirt? Thanks for the money for buying it but your interpretive dance could do with some work because it wasn't clear what was going on.

Lastly yes they have got big crowds and fair play to them for attracting them back but they were fairly quiet for the majority of the game. I was expecting big things really and it would have been good if we hadn't have been so shit so we could have had a bit of singing contest or whatever. After the game I experienced an odd atmosphere among their fans.

Coming out of BP you come across real salt of the earth type people, swearing, occasionally arguments and disagreements etc. Coming out of the ground amongst their fans today I could have been in Tescos. Nothing I heard then would indicate football fans to me. We are a completely different type of person to them generally. I prefer our hardier, more partisan way.

Things were now looking very serious. Grimsby had hit third bottom and it was increasingly looking like three of the bottom two would go down. Town had still not won for 18 games. The upcoming games against Chesterfield and Barnet, both at Blundell Park, were going to be massive.

Pos	Team	P	W	D	L	F	A	GD	Pts
1	Accrington	37	23	5	9	64	40	+24	74
2	Luton	38	20	11	7	79	40	+39	71
3	Notts County	38	18	12	8	60	39	+21	66
4	Wycombe	37	19	9	9	70	52	+18	66
5	Mansfield	37	16	15	6	56	38	+18	63
6	Coventry	37	18	7	12	43	31	+12	61
7	Lincoln	37	16	12	9	53	40	+13	60
8	Exeter	36	18	6	12	46	40	+6	60
9	Swindon	37	19	3	15	58	55	+3	60
10	Carlisle	38	15	11	12	55	48	+7	56
11	Newport County	37	13	14	10	47	47	0	53
12	Crawley Town	37	15	8	14	44	46	-2	53
13	Colchester	37	13	12	12	46	43	+3	51
14	Cambridge	38	13	11	14	38	50	-12	50
15	Cheltenham	38	11	12	15	53	54	-1	45
16	Stevenage	37	11	11	15	50	55	-5	44
17	Yeovil	37	11	9	17	47	57	-10	42
18	Morecambe	36	9	12	15	37	47	-10	39
19	Port Vale	37	9	11	17	41	53	-12	38
20	Crewe	37	11	4	22	44	61	-17	37
21	Forest Green	37	10	7	20	44	64	-20	37
22	Grimsby	38	9	10	19	32	57	-25	37
23	Chesterfield	36	8	7	21	37	65	-28	31
24	Barnet	38	7	9	22	34	56	-22	30

League Table 18th March

WEEK 46

Town got thumped 4-0 at Coventry, with a second-half capitulation seeing the home side romp home from a 1-0 half-time lead.

Chicaneuk: What pisses me off the most is that we had some good spells and looked like we could have had a goal or two. The result flattered Coventry. Sure, they were better than us, but for good portions of the game we gave as good as we got.

Balthazar Bullitt: The first 45 left me thinking that there was enough in the team to win a game.

The collapse in the second half just made me wish the season was over so we can release this team of eunuchs.

The anti-Fenty rants resumed with some big hitters joining the chorus of disapproval directed at the Town director and his fellow board members.

BIGChris: I rarely post on here these days but I have received messages regarding some of the recent posts and debates.

I have to say I still have so much anger about the way GTFC is being run as I mistakenly thought we would ensure the previous errors of judgement would never repeat themselves yet, if anything, the supporter engagement is even worse than it was in 2010. Supporters are treated as idiots with nothing to offer but their admission money.

As others have said, so many long-term fans have had enough, you can only be slapped in the face so many times before either walking away or fighting back.

Given that grim choice which one will you do?

Walking away after decades of total commitment sounds easier than I think it will be. Why should the attachment, the camaraderie, the love for what is often your childhood sweetheart be taken away by someone who may have lost any respect for, primarily because your commitment is not only unappreciated, but laughed at.

Standing up and fighting back takes time, energy and drive and comes with no guarantees of success, however that is measured.

At this moment in time, I don't think I can walk away and desert my club so what can I do?

I, and several others, put in a lot of time and energy into revitalising the Trust. I hold my hands up and tell the world that I had a keen aim to have fan representation on the board of GTFC. I wanted the fans voice to be at heard and I often said that I believed that we were better sat at the boardroom table than stood in the car park throwing stones. I was also of the view that the Trust representative should not be the Trust chair because I felt it more important to retain an independence.

I held the view that we were better off on the club board, even after the time when I left the Trust. The reasons for my departure have largely remained private and that is because I have always believed you don't air your dirty washing in public. I would say that the people who I worked with during my time on the Trust board had my total respect for a thankless task. It is to their credit that some of those stalwarts survive some six or seven years later. Let's just say my reasons were primarily related to the person who is attracting more criticism than he has ever done!

That leads me to express my disappointment at some of the posts over the last few days which have, in my opinion, been unnecessary and personal. We don't always agree, that's good and beneficial, but to accuse people who give up significant amounts of time and energy to try and improve our club as being in it for their own interests is terribly unfair, again, in my opinion.

The way forward now is to back the manager and players for the remaining games in the hope we can avoid relegation. Please note I am not telling anyone to get behind the team, that is not my place to do so, but I will ASK everyone who can to support the players because that is all we can do.

Once our fate is sealed then action must be taken. I hope the Trust will canvass their members with the question about giving up the seat on the club board. Whether we stay up or not the fans will demand change and the vehicle to do that has to be the Trust. If the members wish to give up the seat then it is likely the bars will be handed back to the club. Sad but necessary in my view

If JF will not change then the fans must unite to effect removal.

This course of action is sad and an awful situation to be in but for me, doing nothing and continuing as we are is not an option, unless you wish to walk away without a murmur. That may happen but season ticket sales will slump without boardroom change.

Personally I don't think there is any need for a breakaway Trust, what we may need is to get the people with energy and drive for change to join together to unite the fan base with the aim of being professional and bringing about a brighter future for GTFC. Doing nothing after May 2018 is not an option IMO.

Caesar. I was willing to forgive Fenty a lot. Our time in non-league was partly his fault of course, but I always imagined how much it haunted him that that had happened on his watch. I looked at awful owners elsewhere and thought at least Fenty isn't them.

TO HELL AND BACK

But since coming back to the league his every action seems to have been in direct contradiction to all the supposed lessons I thought we had learnt in non-league.

The fans and the club were united, pushing in the same direction. Wanting to build on the success of promotion. Then there is no push or incentive to drive up season ticket sales, he votes for b-teams then maintains radio silence for as long as possible showing no care for how to communicate with fans. Fails to fight to keep Hurst, and while to be fair I felt Bignot was a good appointment at the time the sacking of hin and subsequent appointment of Slade was handled appallingly. Any pretending to listen to fans goes out the window as this season becomes a catalogue of mistakes, voting for b-teams again and that risible statement blaming the EFL for not explaining it better. After a first decent statement maintaining silence after Stevenage, picking a fight with a local journalist and making a fans forum turn into a farce and a chance to gang up on them. Disrespecting and effectively firing a volunteer SLO that had been one of the few bright spots. Putting out statement after statement backing Slade as he allowed any creative player to be sold off and all the people who had any connection with the fans to be sold off and replaced by loanees and useless mercenaries. Now he thinks OP was a burden for the club, well in the nearly 20 years he has been there he talks about his 2 million of 'benign' loans. We in one season put £100,000 into the club with no return demanded, aside from the money we put in season after season to watch, buy merchandise and be part of our club. Enough is enough. To go to conference once would be forgivable. Twice shows that there is incompetence somewhere and as much as he wants to blame the fans he can't on this one. All his actions suggests he just doesn't think of fans as stakeholders of the club.

It feels like everyone sees it now, I consider myself a latecomer to this conclusion but it seems clear now and has been for some time, our club will continue to be stuck in a malaise like this until Fenty leaves, and most of the board with him.

***Hagrid** It's over. And you John have done it. You should be ashamed. I couldn't give a shit if I get bollocked for this, the one bit of joy I've had in my time supporting Town was Wembley 16 when we got back to the EFL. You and the board with your penny pinching your cost-cutting your hopeless appointment and persistence with Slade and Wilkinson. 2 fuckwits who haven't a clue. It's over John, we are finished. The fans have gone. No one NO ONE believes we are staying up. The feeble "stick with us" issued out by the drones each week, we don't want to fucking hear it. We've had it, we've had enough. No matter if we do stay up, do you really think the fans are going to come flooding back? You've ruined everything we achieved through promotion. And when we go down next month John, believe me, you won't see me or 2000 others back, because you don't deserve us, we are taken for granted, treated like shit, and for what? For our team to be humiliated week in week out. Had enough. Fuck me I pray we can survive, I really do, but it's not happening. This time John, we won't come back.*

Chesterfield's win meant they could now overtake Town if they won just one of their games in hand, with the Mariners having an inferior goal difference. Grimsby were just about in charge of their own destiny as they still had to play both Chesterfield and Barnet at home. But with 19 winless games under three different managers, it was hard to see Town beating anyone.

Pos	Team	P	W	D	L	F	A	GD	Pts
1	Luton	39	21	11	7	81	40	+41	74
2	Accrington	37	23	5	9	64	40	+24	74
3	Wycombe	39	20	10	9	73	54	+19	70
4	Notts County	39	18	12	9	61	42	+19	66
5	Exeter	38	20	6	12	50	41	+9	66
6	Coventry	38	19	7	12	47	31	+16	64
7	Mansfield	38	16	15	7	56	40	+16	63
8	Lincoln	38	16	13	9	53	40	+13	61
9	Swindon	38	19	3	16	59	58	+1	60
10	Carlisle	39	15	12	12	56	49	+7	57
11	Colchester	39	14	13	12	47	43	+4	55
12	Newport County	38	13	14	11	48	49	-1	53
13	Crawley Town	39	15	8	16	49	54	-5	53
14	Cambridge	39	13	12	14	39	51	-12	51
15	Cheltenham	39	12	12	15	58	57	+1	48
16	Stevenage	38	11	11	16	50	56	-6	44
17	Crewe	39	13	4	22	49	63	-14	43
18	Yeovil	37	11	9	17	47	57	-10	42
19	Morecambe	38	9	14	15	37	47	-10	41
20	Forest Green	39	11	7	21	47	67	-20	40
21	Port Vale	39	9	12	18	41	54	-13	39
22	Grimsby	39	9	10	20	32	61	-29	37
23	Chesterfield	37	9	7	21	40	66	-26	34
24	Barnet	39	7	9	23	34	58	-24	30

League Table 25th March

WEEK 47

The enquiry into the trouble at the Port Vale game mainly blamed alcohol and the club decided to alter their serving times - and ban anyone deemed to be responsible.
Link: https://www.grimsby-townfc.co.uk/news/2018/march/club-statement/

Darren9: *The biggest issue with the problems against Port Vale was the club not paying to have police in the ground. This is despite the obvious intelligence held by the police who had increased their presence in the area during the build-up to the game.*

The statement from the club makes no reference to this and while I accept that football should be free from these issues I also know that it isn't and failure to take the necessary steps leads to scenes like the ones we saw.

The blaming of fans and the suggestion that it was alcohol-fuelled shows a basic lack of understanding of the problems encountered on that day and those that will be encountered in the future. Alcohol may have had a small influence on the events but it was not the main issue. The issue was that a certain element from Port Vale travelled and were not correctly policed once inside the ground, and that our risk element were also not effectively controlled. Disorder would have occurred if alcohol was not sold in the ground.

It is easy to blame the supporters. To suggest that they are mindless thugs who need to be treated as such but it's not the case. A small number of the crowd on that particular day were intent on causing disorder in the ground. The way to combat this would be either to have police in the ground or to have the right number of correctly trained stewards in the ground. Neither of which happened and allowed the disorder to take place.

Punishing all fans is just another example of how out of touch those who run our football club are.

Good Friday saw the first of two massive games at Easter and Town desperately needed a win.

Jonnyboy82: *If we don't win on Friday then for me it's all over even this early on, we need to win this match but the thing is we haven't won for nearly 20 games so I just can't see it.*

> I think it's over I really do.
>
> Thank you Russell Slade for leaving us with pure shit and thank you John Fenty for ruining our season for selling our best players and appointing a man you should never have appointed.
>
> I'm sat here so depressed and thinking what was he thinking.
>
> **Heisenberg**: I'd say that if we don't beat Stevenage on Friday, then it's over. It doesn't matter what the other scores are this weekend, anything other than a win and I fear we're down. The table won't look a complete lost cause to the general public who don't really understand our current predicament, no matter how this weekend goes, but if we can't beat Stevenage, we won't beat the other teams either (especially Wycombe and Swindon).
>
> To stay up with an 18+ game winless run sandwiched anywhere in your season would be an absolute miracle, and I can't see it happening.
>
> I really hope I'm wrong, but you'd need a huge amount of blind faith to ignore our current form and think we're going to turn it around any time soon. There is absolutely no rule that says we'll win any of the remaining games, it's quite conceivable we'll start the 2018/19 season down in the Conference and without a win in the whole of 2018. What a thought.

Unfortunately, Town drew 0-0 with Stevenage at Blundell Park. It wasn't a disaster thanks to other results, but the results still left the Mariners at the mercy of Chesterfield.

The fans picked on the Slade players, but at least new signing Fox was beginning to make an impression, at least for some fans.

> **davmariner**: FUCK YOU SLADE. Getting rid of any creative players we had. Clements, Jones, Bolarinwa, Osborne. FUCK YOU.
>
> **Hagrid** I hope I don't see [Mitch] Rose in a Town shirt again
>
> **Mighty_Mariner**: I've not seen much mentioned about Andrew Fox since his arrival but in my opinion deserves a thread of his own as I think he's been superb, especially yesterday.

Perhaps because he seems to be the anti-Paul Dixon I don't know but he's been a solid performer in the two games I've seen. He's full-blooded, got good energy, decent touch, control and pass, can carry the ball forward well and importantly, can defend well.

I'd be more than happy to see his retain the left-back berth next season, regardless of which league we're in.

All the more annoying that we had him on trial in the summer and let him go!

Balaby*: Rose and Hooper are probably the worst two players I've witnessed in a Town shirt in last 20 years!!!*

How these players earn a living from being professional footballers is a disgrace. It boils my blood to watch players like these pull on a shirts for us!!! Bereft of any footballing know-how or skill of any kind. Even if they put the effort in you could forgive them for some of their failings, but to watch them perform how they did today when 5000 fans turn up wanting the team to give their all to make sure this great club survives in the Football League and witness what effort they put in today is unforgivable!!!

If this is all we can offer there's only one outcome!!!

Hopefully the teams below us somehow perform worse than what we can offer!!! But surely that's impossible!!! UTM

The Old Codger: *At least McAllister is ready for Monday*

The point against Stevenage, for the first time in weeks, had left Grimsby better off than the day before, mainly because Chesterfield had lost. Barnet were gaining ground though and they undoubtedly had the best run-in on paper of all the bottom sides.

Pos	Team	P	W	D	L	F	A	GD	Pts
1	Accrington	38	24	5	9	65	40	+25	77
2	Luton	40	21	11	8	82	42	+40	74
3	Wycombe	40	20	11	9	73	54	+19	71
4	Notts County	40	18	13	9	61	42	+19	67
5	Exeter	39	20	6	13	52	44	+8	66
6	Coventry	39	19	8	12	48	32	+16	65
7	Lincoln	39	17	13	9	56	42	+14	64
8	Mansfield	39	16	15	8	56	41	+15	63
9	Swindon	39	19	4	16	60	59	+1	61
10	Carlisle	40	16	12	12	57	49	+8	60
11	Colchester	40	15	13	12	49	44	+5	58
12	Newport County	39	13	15	11	49	50	-1	54
13	Cambridge	40	14	12	14	42	52	-10	54
14	Crawley Town	40	15	8	17	50	57	-7	53
15	Cheltenham	40	12	12	16	58	58	0	48
16	Stevenage	39	11	12	16	50	56	-6	45
17	Crewe	40	13	4	23	50	65	-15	43
18	Yeovil	37	11	9	17	47	57	-10	42
19	Morecambe	39	9	15	15	38	48	-10	42
20	Port Vale	40	10	12	18	43	55	-12	42
21	Forest Green	39	11	7	21	47	67	-20	40
22	Grimsby	40	9	11	20	32	61	-29	38
23	Chesterfield	38	9	7	22	41	68	-27	34
24	Barnet	40	8	9	23	36	59	-23	33

League Table 1st April

WEEK 48

Grimsby took the lead at Wycombe then conceded two second-half goals to come away win nothing. Town fans were disappointed but not downbeat after an improved showing.

TO HELL AND BACK

LondonMariner43: From a much improved and promising performance, just 2-3 months too late (thanks Fenty). Wycombe are a decent side massive attacking threat with the unplayable Akinfemwa pace and trickery down the side ,competent midfield and 2 tough centre-halves who knew every trick in the book. I'd hate to see the possession stats as they looked threatening every time they went forward and to be honest on another day they could've had 5 or 6. We did well to hold the lead for as long as we did and at least we didn't cave in having conceded two quick goals. Rose who was my MOTM fluffed a great chance to equalise after 80 but I always felt that Wycombe would've just upped it again and found a way through. McKeown made domed great saves and the defence was valiant to a man throwing themselves into challenges and block.in midfield rose n summerfield were everywhere, but the problem is that they and the rest of the team just don't have the quality to create things. Vernon is the same whilst Matt and Hooper never looked like they thought they could win a header or create a chance. Woolford took his goal well but was anonymous as was Berrett, who was up to his usual standard. We couldn't really have done anything more but the sad fact is that our best just isn't good enough. Even McSheffery when he came on managed to stand on the ball and fail to beat the first man with his corners and he's supposed to be our one bit of quality.

And the other depressing thought is that most of these players will be gone and don't look good enough even for the conference.

Let's just hope Chesterfield have a bad day and that we can put in a similar level of performance. In which case we might have a chance

Finally, special thanks to the myopic ref who might as well have donned a blue shirt and tried to head one in for them. They were far too clever with their pushing and pulling and we were too amateurish in our shoves and nudges.

cod_head_doug: Having got over the euphoria of taking the lead in a match for the first time in ages, and then the disappointment of losing the game, I think it is time in retrospect to look at the reasons why I believe we will stay up.

Since Mike Jolley has taken over there is now a plan and a purpose about the team.

Mike is ambitious and wants to succeed.
The players are definitely playing for him.
The work rate has improved from the majority of the team.
Our tactics, especially in the first half, are improving.
The joy that the players showed when we scored showed what it meant to them, as did the dejection at the final whistle.
Wycombe resorted to time wasting, a few cynical fouls and cheating to hold on to the win.
We stopped Akinfenwa from scoring for the first time.
We had them rattled when Martin Woolford scored.

We scored a goal from open play.
We scored a goal!!!!
We created some excellent chances to score.
The players were out on their feet at the end.
We will win on Saturday................it is written........it has all been leading up to this.
I don't want Slade's legacy to be relegation.
We're all Town aren't we?
Same again, landlord!!
Macca was excellent, that double save near the end was worth the travel on its own.

HertsGTFC *Overall a better performance and a well-taken goal from open play! Let's not forget Wycombe are 3rd for a reason and that reason is that they are well organised and play to their strengths, all that said we deserved a point today despite the ref doing his best to deny us.*

In the first half I am not sure if we were the better team, but the lead was well deserved with the players showing real grit and determination as well as actually trying to play some football. When we came out for the 2nd half we failed to win and retain possession enough to build on the lead, you could sense that their first was coming but the 2nd I'm not sure they deserved. We did have enough possession in the right areas to force an equaliser. Rose came frustratingly close and if Matt had squared to McSheffery things might have been different.

So overall, we didn't look like a relegation side and if we had seen today's effort and application 6 weeks ago we would both be where we are. MJ won't turn this around but given time he will improve us.

Gareth Ainsworth [Wycombe manager] showed some real class at the end when he came towards the Town fans clapping and signalling that we will be staying up, he didn't need to do that but it was nice to see either way.

Buckstown *Well that was my first game in a while and I went in hope rather than expectation. I have to say it was better than I expected and most importantly the players gave everything and very clearly care, the problem is we're just not good enough, particularly in midfield.*

Wycombe are one dimensional, get it to Akinfenwa who either wins the header and Wycombe win the second ball, or chest it down and lay it off. The balls into him were delivered with laser-guided accuracy and he does exactly what it says on the tin, highly effectively. We had Vernon and latterly Matt who both work hard but win little or nothing

Rose was not good, jumping out of tackles and finally missing a sitter near the end. Summerfield worked very hard and was encouraging the others throughout but he was alone in midfield. Woolford won a number of balls in the air which surprised me but offered little else.

TO HELL AND BACK

My biggest fear was that we would be hopeless and I would leave thinking Jolley is a big mistake. Instead I left thinking he's getting almost the maximum out of a bunch of dogs. I do think he needs to pick his best eleven and play them for the remaining games to maximise our chance of survival.

Credit to Gareth Ainsworth who has performed miracles at Wycombe on a pitiful budget. He also applauded the Town fans at the end which was a nice touch

Any suggestion that MJ was to blame seemed to be dismissed. The blame for Town's predicament lay elsewhere:

Chicaneuk *(replying to another post): Sorry mate but this is nonsense. We lead the game for the first half and ultimately gave a fairly good account of ourselves.*

I'm not disputing we're in the shit and we need some results desperately now but we didn't give a bad account of ourselves today and in isolation, if the situation weren't so dire, we probably would have expected this (or worse) result.

No disrespect but sheer desperation and frustration with our position is making some posters on here lose their grip on reality, in terms of managing expectations.

monkeyboy: *MJ is in no way shape or form to blame for any of this, he should have the full backing from every fan until his own team is installed and the crap we have is gone.*

The main people to blame are as follows: - Slade, Clarke, all the midfield barring McAllister, and all the attack. The rest ain't too bad.

The Old Codger: *The main people to blame are:- Fenty, Marley, Chapman & Day. They appointed Slade when we were doing OK.*

The big one against Chesterfield was just around the corner. Town had not won for 20 games but suddenly they had a match they could not afford to lose! Many fans were resigned to going down, others were already looking for someone to blame, no guesses who.

Mariner91: *The inquest can start no matter what league we're in. Fenty out.*

Spireite1866: *Spireite here in peace.*

I'm not normally one to visit opposing team's message boards but due to the gravity of Saturday's fixture, curiosity got the better of me.

It seems there's a club in as much turmoil, both on and off the pitch, as my own.

Off the pitch, we've been riddled with scandal and are constantly being told our debt is rising and the current owner, who wants nothing more to do with us, is being forced into chucking cash in every month just to keep us in business. We're not quite sure what happened to the substantial transfer fees received for Darikwa (to Burnley), Morsy (to Barnsley), Clucas (Hull for 1.2m then sell-on received from his 16m move to Swansea), Doyle (to Cardiff), Cooper (to Leeds) plus Paul Cook compo when he left for Pompey. Need I go on? Our club has been stripped and is on a cliff's edge.

On the pitch. Not much better really. Jack Lester is a club legend but he's taken on one hell of a task.

We are certainly a side capable of some lovely football and we've got, arguably, the best goalscorer in the division. Dennis has the thick end of 20 goals this term in a struggling side.

On the flip side, we have the softest underbelly and we've been bullied out of games time and time again this year.

Injuries have been a huge part of our demise this season but we've shown no heart or desire on far too many occasions and I fear this could be the case Saturday.

I honestly think we are the only side on Saturday that is capable of winning the game but I know far too well that we are more than capable of losing the game by rolling over.

I cannot wish you well for Saturday but I genuinely do not wish to see Grimsby leave the league. I'd much rather be playing yourselves than the likes of Forest Green, Crawley and Yeovil.

Unfortunately, I think it's us or you.

Whatever happens I wish GTFC all the best moving forward with sorting their club out.

Not much had changed at the bottom over Good Friday, with Barnet and Grimsby both losing. Chesterfield's match with Newport had been postponed so they had an extra game in hand.

Pos	Team	P	W	D	L	F	A	GD	Pts
1	Accrington	39	25	5	9	66	40	+26	80
2	Luton	41	22	11	8	84	43	+41	77
3	Wycombe	41	21	11	9	75	55	+20	74
4	Exeter	40	21	6	13	54	45	+9	69
5	Notts County	41	18	13	10	61	43	+18	67
6	Lincoln	40	18	13	9	57	42	+15	67
7	Coventry	40	19	8	13	50	38	+12	65
8	Mansfield	40	16	15	9	57	43	+14	63
9	Swindon	40	19	5	16	61	60	+1	62
10	Colchester	41	16	13	12	51	45	+6	61
11	Carlisle	41	16	12	13	57	50	+7	60
12	Newport County	39	13	15	11	49	50	-1	54
13	Crawley Town	41	15	9	17	51	58	-7	54
14	Cambridge	40	14	12	14	42	52	-10	54
15	Cheltenham	41	12	12	17	59	60	-1	48
16	Stevenage	40	12	12	16	54	57	-3	48
17	Yeovil	38	12	9	17	53	59	-6	45
18	Crewe	41	13	5	23	52	67	-15	44
19	Port Vale	41	10	13	18	45	57	-12	43
20	Morecambe	39	9	15	15	38	48	-10	42
21	Forest Green	40	11	7	22	48	69	-21	40
22	Grimsby	41	9	11	21	33	63	-30	38
23	Chesterfield	38	9	7	22	41	68	-27	34
24	Barnet	41	8	9	24	37	63	-26	33

League Table 1st April

APRIL

The Resurrection

WEEK 48 (CONTINUED)

Finally, the game that Town could not afford to lose came along, Chesterfield at home. Grimsby had got away to some extent with all the points dropped in the "must-win" games so far, but this was a game they just could not afford to lose. Even a draw didn't look enough as Chesterfield and Barnet looked to have easier run-ins.

Amazingly Town won the "must-win" game thanks to a late penalty scored in front of the Pontoon under intense pressure from Mitch Rose. The Mariners were far from safe, but things looked a lot better. The relief was palpable.

Codcheeky: *A big congratulations to MJ on his first win in the EFL, hopefully it is the start of good times ahead.*

Smokey111: *Two poor sides huffing and puffing but we huffed and puffed a bit more! Special mention for Woolford. He's had a lot of stick but him and Rose both performed well. UTM.*

OneLove: *I thought yesterday was all-round incredible, the sound system was bang on, the tunes were bang on. The ref showed a total difference from these clueless lower league ones, the fans were mega, the team put in an excellent shift and that at the end showed what it meant with the buzz from all the crowd and the players. We go again next Sat and can put it to bed. Still on cloud nine now, big up everyone. Up the fooking Mariners!*

toontown: *I am surprised that we are seeing the typical overreaction to a win. We were most definitely not fantastic defensively. Chesterfield didn't hurt us, to be fair we kept them under control, but we repeatedly made awful individual fuck-ups and presented them with the ball. Mostly in the first half, but the worst occasion was from Clarke in the second half. Luckily, we were playing against such an awful team.*

TO HELL AND BACK

We had good performances from midfield in the middle third but yet again there was no creativity. Up front we did have a couple of chances such as when Hooper was presented with a 1 on 1, but spurned them yet again.

I am glad that MJ seems to be getting us organised defensively at home, but nothing can cover up the awful individual lack of ability running through this team from front to back. Thank God there are only a few games left so this win may be enough.

No lack of effort from the team today, don't get me wrong, and we had some individual decent performances, but you can still see why we are where we are.

TheGoalKipper (in reply): Are you serious? How long is it since we won? Never mind the importance of this game which everyone admits we had to win. We have just given ourselves a chance of escaping the trapdoor to non-league and you say this because we are overjoyed that we now have hope.

If we survive we know there is a lot of work to do for next season but there is nothing we can do about that. Sometimes just being alive has to be enough.

ginnywings: See what you are saying toontown, but we are down the bottom for a reason, same as Chesterfield. We weren't great but we were better than them and deserved to win. We only have to match the other crap sides in the league now and we will be safe. I expect there will be many more mistakes before the season is over, but Barnet and FGR will make a few as well. I'm just rejoicing in the 3 points and the momentum it gives us. I don't care about the performance.

AndyDarloFC. I had a top weekend with some top lads. I am paying for it on this train home now.

It was a fantastic 3 points for you boys. Must be my good luck haha.

You're safe now. You'll hammer Barnet next week. See yous all at Forest Green.

The Chesterfield fan who posted before the game was gutted.

Spireite1866. Congratulations on most probably preserving your league status yesterday.

You can hopefully appreciate how bad we've had it as well this season, we are absolutely awful on far too many occasions.

I stand by my initial thought that we were the only ones capable of winning the game during the first half. We created two or three very good chances and hats off to your keeper for the brilliant save denying Dennis towards the end of the first half.

Second half, however, we lost the game. We had no heart or desire, absolutely no quality and credit to your side for wanting it more and totally winning the second half.

I've not brought myself to look at the penalty decision again but from what I hear at our end, stone wall and no argument whatsoever.

It's not over but the fat lady is getting hydrated and warming herself up.

Best of luck going forward with sorting out your own ownership issues and hopefully we'll meet again soon. In the Football League.

On a side note, interesting take on the Family Stand at Blundell Park. They young-uns are a bit lively!

Long term though many supporters were still doubtful about, well, whether to keep supporting the team (at least to the ultimate extent of investing in a season ticket).

---

headingly_mariner: *I am a season ticket holder and it's not about the level of football for me. I was a STH all the way through our drop from the Championship and throughout the Conference years. I don't mind if we are shite, I still want to attend because Grimsby Town are my team and I don't like it when I am not at games.*

I live out of Town, having a ST is a tie to my hometown and I see my ageing Grandparents regularly because I am often in town for the football. I have often used that as an excuse to renew previously.

This time is a bit different, I am desperately upset with the way the club is run, I felt particularly insulted over the Checkatrade bullying issue, the board views on Operation Promotion and the general disregard for fan feelings. I have long been critical of the board and continued to attend. I am not sure I can do that anymore. I will not be giving up going because I can't be arsed or I am not being entertained or we get relegated, If that was the case I'd have given up years ago and it will break my heart not to be at Blundell Park when we are playing.

If I decide not to go it will be because I feel attending only justifies John Fenty and the board's position in control of the club. It's a long way to the start of the season and it's a decision I will struggle to make, I am just fed up of having the piss taking out of me by the board.

I would like to see them publicly accept responsibility for the mess, commit to writing loans off and leaving the club debt-free whatever division we are in. I can't imagine this will happen, I think we will lose a 1000 STH's and the club will continue dying a slow death.

The match with Chesterfield was undoubtedly a game changer and the league table looked very different as a result. The Spirites now looked doomed but Barnet were starting to look like they might escape. Barnet still had Grimsby and Chesterfield to play. Should they win them both then Town would need something from the games against Swindon and Notts County, or it would all go down to the final game away at Forest Green. Nobody wanted a repeat of the final day of the season at Burton in 2010 when the Mariners had been relegated from the Football League.

Pos	Team	P	W	D	L	F	A	GD	Pts
1	Accrington	40	26	5	9	67	40	+27	83
2	Luton	42	23	11	8	87	43	+44	80
3	Wycombe	41	21	11	9	75	55	+20	74
4	Exeter	41	22	6	13	57	47	+10	72
5	Notts County	42	19	13	10	63	44	+19	70
6	Lincoln	40	18	13	9	57	42	+15	67
7	Coventry	41	19	8	14	51	40	+11	65
8	Mansfield	41	16	15	10	60	47	+13	63
9	Swindon	41	19	6	16	61	60	+1	63
10	Carlisle	42	16	13	13	57	50	+7	61
11	Colchester	42	16	13	13	51	46	+5	61
12	Crawley Town	42	16	9	17	53	59	-6	57
13	Newport County	40	13	15	12	49	51	-2	54
14	Cambridge	41	14	12	15	44	55	-11	54
15	Cheltenham	42	13	12	17	62	60	+2	51
16	Stevenage	41	13	12	16	55	57	-2	51
17	Crewe	42	14	5	23	56	70	-14	47
18	Yeovil	39	12	9	18	53	62	-9	45
19	Port Vale	42	10	13	19	46	59	-13	43
20	Morecambe	40	9	15	16	38	51	-13	42
21	Grimsby	42	10	11	21	34	63	-29	41
22	Forest Green	41	11	7	23	48	70	-22	40
23	Barnet	42	9	9	24	38	63	-25	36
24	Chesterfield	39	9	7	23	41	69	-28	34

League Table 7th April

WEEK 49

With a win against Chesterfield under their belts, Town faced another "must win" game against Barnet. A win would mean safety, a loss grave danger, and a draw somewhere in between.

---

ginnywings (on contemplating whether a draw would be enough). Isn't it tiresome thinking about it? Studying the league table and the fixtures, wondering if a draw at home against a very poor Barnet side will be enough to squeeze us over the line. Hoping and praying that other crap sides lose to give us a bit of a boost. Never have I wanted a season to end as quickly as this one.

With Town having a winning record over most of the teams around them, most posters did not agree with the suggestion that Goal Difference was unfair and "Head to Head" should be used instead, as in many other countries, as a tie-breaker for teams on equal points.

Pizzzza (replying to another post): I disagree, a league is played over 46 games and goal difference is a better and fairer indicator of performance over the entire season.

The days building up to the game were full of speculation about what might happen, and how many fans would be there.

---

ginnywings. I must say I'm a bit surprised and more than a little disappointed there are no offers on for this weekend to pack the park. I just don't get it and the crowd will be down significantly from the last game, without all those away fans and those that turned up for free/cheap for the last two games. If they think a disco set from your worst nightmare wedding reception is going to suffice, I think they are making a huge miscalculation.

I really don't get the thinking behind our board. So much but no more seems to be their modus operandi. Something that worked so well for the last 2 home games has just been abandoned, with arguably a bigger game than Chesterfield coming up.

Poor!

Mighty Mariner, the club mascot for many years, returned for the Barnet game after a long time in exile, stemming from a disagreement between him and the club, which had now been settled. It was good to have him back!

Abdul19: What's the obsession with bringing back former mascots? For me, Clive, we need to be looking at bringing in fresh ideas; either a mascot who's worked his way up through the leagues, or one with a pro licence that's looking to make the move away from academy football.

Meanwhile the news that no bans would be given to the Vale fans that went on the pitch, but Town fans who had done the same *would* get a ban, was judged to be unfair and illogical.

Mimma: No banning orders for the Vale "fans" that went on the pitch. Double standards, ban our own fans, every other team's fans get away with it.

Inevitably the Barnet game ended in a draw, after Town took the lead, then fell behind, with Mitch Rose once again doing the business from the penalty spot. That meant Grimsby missed the chance to save themselves.

Chrisblor: None of our outfield players have the composure to score from open play. Cardwell and Clifton were both guilty of spannering over very decent chances to score. I have to say given this Jolley has done very well to make us more of a threat from set-pieces (I'm including throw-ins and penalties here).

Ultimately it has to be a confidence thing. I really don't think the crowd did the players any favours at all this afternoon. In the Upper there were plenty falling over themselves to loudly abuse our players after they made mistakes. Has everyone forgotten they're not world-beaters? We didn't win for 20 games! Of course, they'll mess up but the crowd getting on their backs instead of supporting them I think contributed a lot towards our nervous performance in the second half.

I also have to say it was noticeable how one of our starting strikers got far more abuse than the other, which was interesting given I personally thought they put in similarly effective performances today. I wonder why that could be....

MJ's post-match comments were jumped upon, positively for once.

Mariner93er: *Is it possible to set us up convincingly with the players at our disposal?*

The much-maligned JJ Hooper was starting to attract some praise, although not everyone had been won over.

grimsby pete: *Michael Jolley told the Telegraph he is pleased with the response from the said two after a lot of criticism from the fans. Well done to both keep it up lads.*

gtfc98: *Did Hooper respond though? He still looked nothing other than lazy to me. Rose showed great character and composure to put the penalty away though.*

TheRealJohnLewis: *Yes, he did, the front two ran their socks off and never stopped chasing.*

Meanwhile the drum of underlying discontent from the most outspoken critics kept pounding in the background.

Grimsbys finest *I'm pleased to see that people are holding off at the minute but as soon as our fate is sealed then our voices of discontent must be heard.*

Town needed 2 points from the last 3 games. The first two however were quite tricky, against Notts County and Swindon, both hoping to be promoted. Only the last game at Forest Green looked winnable, but everyone would prefer the points sooner rather than later. The best bet looked to be Barnet to drop points, although all their games were against sides at the bottom of the table.

Pos	Team	P	W	D	L	F	A	GD	Pts
1	Accrington	41	26	6	9	68	41	+27	84
2	Luton	43	24	11	8	90	44	+46	83
3	Wycombe	42	22	11	9	76	55	+21	77
4	Notts County	43	20	13	10	66	45	+21	73
5	Exeter	42	22	7	13	58	48	+10	73
6	Coventry	42	20	8	14	53	41	+12	68
7	Mansfield	43	17	16	10	62	48	+14	67
8	Lincoln	41	18	13	10	57	43	+14	67
9	Swindon	43	19	7	17	64	64	0	64
10	Carlisle	43	16	14	13	58	51	+7	62
11	Colchester	43	16	13	14	52	49	+3	61
12	Newport County	41	14	15	12	51	52	-1	57
13	Crawley Town	43	16	9	18	54	61	-7	57
14	Cambridge	42	15	12	15	46	55	-9	57
15	Stevenage	43	13	13	17	56	60	-4	52
16	Cheltenham	43	13	12	18	62	61	+1	51
17	Crewe	43	14	5	24	57	73	-16	47
18	Yeovil	41	12	10	19	55	65	-10	46
19	Port Vale	43	11	13	19	47	59	-12	46
20	Morecambe	42	9	17	16	41	54	-13	44
21	Forest Green	42	12	7	23	49	70	-21	43
22	Grimsby	43	10	12	21	36	65	-29	42
23	Barnet	43	9	10	24	40	65	-25	37
24	Chesterfield	41	9	8	24	43	72	-29	35

League Table 15th April

WEEK 50

With all the bottom teams playing one another seemingly every week the possibilities were endless, but that didn't stop fans from trying to work them out. The best bet though seemed Barnet to lose one of their games and it was almost guaranteed Town would be safe. It seemed like Town's fate was more in other's hands than it was in their own.

Mariner91: *I am not sure why people are so down on our chances of getting points compared to how they think Barnet will fare. Notts County are such a good team that they lost 3-1 to the only side we've managed to beat since December and looked absolutely dreadful in that game. If they're out of the automatic picture by then and rest players, we could potentially get a result.*

And Swindon are the team in worst form in the division. They're only seven points ahead of Newport having played two games more and are in much worse form, yet people are seemingly of the opinion that we've no chance of getting anything against them whilst a home win for Barnet against Newport is a foregone conclusion.

Both us and Barnet are rubbish teams which is why we're in the positions we are in. Barnet have won less than one game out of every four so I'd say it's highly unlikely they'll win all three of their remaining fixtures and even reasonably unlikely that they'll win two of their last three. If we can get two points, which is not impossible, then I think we'll be safe.

TownSNAFU5: *This is worth a thread because we could soon end up confirming our FL place. We need some positivity.*

A win at Swindon (put us on to 45 points) and defeats for Barnet and Chesterfield keep us up. We are due an away win, Swindon are on a poor run of form, they are unlikely to make the play-offs and there are always shocks at the end of a season.

A win at Swindon and 2 draws for Barnet and Chesterfield puts us in a very good position. Barnet cannot catch us and Chesterfield would need to win their last 3 games to pip us on GD. (This also assumes that we do not get any points from our last 2 games. One point would put us safe. Chesterfield playing Barnet on the last day does not make any difference).

A draw at Swindon (we would be on 43 points) and defeats for Barnet and Chesterfield also puts us in a good position. Both Barnet and Chesterfield would need to win all their remaining 5 games to finish above us. A very tall order. Barnet could reach 43 points so we would need another point to be absolutely safe. Chesterfield could reach a maximum of 44 points. It would help if Chesterfield did not win at Barnet on the last day. (Both teams could not finish above, but 1 could).

Ok, lots of ifs and buts for various games. Stranger things have happened though. Visualisation is half the achievement in sport.

TO HELL AND BACK

GrimRob: *On Thursdays and Fridays, I often think we're going to win. It's Saturdays and Sundays which are the problem.*

Grimsby headed to Swindon expecting nothing, and even a point was beyond most fans' wildest dreams given that Swindon needed to win to make the play-offs. The Mariners though amazingly won with Mitch Rose again the hero from the spot and Grimsby unbelievably kept a clean sheet with Macca outstanding in goal. Just two points were needed now to be certain, or Barnet to drop points in either of their final two games. Suddenly there were far more ways for Town to be safe than not to be safe and the ball was firmly in the Mariners' court. Almost overnight it seemed the relegation fears has gone from a distinct possibility to a quite distant one.

Sussexmariner: *Just back to the pub next to Swindon train station. Town were lacking in quality players as we all know but again, all gave 100% for the manager. A great save from Macca mid-way through the 2nd half but really no other clear-cut chances for them, clear handball for their disallowed goal and I thought a clear penalty as their player clipped Cardwell's ankle.*

Great scenes after the final whistle with Jolley and the fans.

A good day to be a Town fan!

HertsGTFC: *Just back, a gritty well-organised performance where the lads worked their socks off to get an essential 3 points. What we lack in quality we made up for in application, work rate and looking at the game sticking to the plan.*

The 4-1- 4-1 works well away from home by the looks of it as despite a top quality save from Macca and them hitting the woodwork, can't remember seeing that TBH I'm not convinced Town looked in too much trouble considering the difference in league position. If we only had more quality and composure in the final 3rd we would not be going through this dogfight.

I've not seen the penalty on anything other than my mobile so far but it looks like shall we say it was "won" by Cardwell. Although the keeper got close to saving it Mitch Rose once again stuck 2 fingers up to those who have suggested he does not care.

The 2nd half was inevitably nervy, not as we were defending for our lives but more about everyone was just waiting for a "typical Town" moment which I'm glad to say never came.

Rob Sedgwick

It appears that the players are responding to having a plan rather than just hoofing it forward Slade ball style.

The players stood up today..........

Macca - Assured, and when required he made a top draw save, again!
RHB - Did o.k. but looked like he was blowing a bit after the break on a hot day
Foxy - As above
Collins - Immense
Clarke - Good
Summers - The performance level we have been used to this season, fit as a flea this lad.
Rose - Good game and once again showed balls of steel
Woolford - Working harder every week and fits well into today's system
Clifton - Well all I can say is that you can see what this means to him, best game yet for Town
Hooper - Keep starting him he will come good sooner or later, all about confidence with this lad.
Cardwell - A great shift from a young lad in the lone role, he does need someone closer to him though.

Subs - Davis brought an experienced cool head, Matt didn't look fit TBH and Suleiman was an odd addition in right midfield, but I guess we won so it doesn't matter.

The Manager - Outwitted the person who if stories are to be believed turned us down.

The fans - Top class as usual away from home and the bit when MJ came over at the end was really good to see, he's still massively learning but one thing he clearly gets is how much it means to us.

Personally, I still think it will go down to the last day but everyone involved with GTFC deserves some credit tonight.

headingly_mariner: *Great effort from the players and a really well-organised away performance.*

If Harry Cardwell can have some quality coached into him and be a bit more composed he could end up being a really useful player. He ran himself out and never gave up on anything, the lad deserves a goal. He does have a real knack for winning pens though.

Mighty_Mariner: *What a great job he's [MJ] done in turning us around.*
It took a few Agnes to get into his stride, get his message into the players but we now look like a well-drilled, organised unit with that won't crumble at the first sign of adversity.

Yes, we still lack a consistent goal threat but he's really tapped into the strengths of the team and worked out a way to make us dangerous to the opposition while staying compact and hard to beat.

He's clearly very tactically astute and as others have said 'gets' what we're all about. We need to follow in Lincoln's footsteps and give him a long-term contract. Let's show our faith in him and display our belief that our long-term future is safe in his hands by giving him a 3-4 year contract. If he can get this shower into a well-organised unit that gets results, imagine what he can do with HIS squad and a full pre-season under his belt.

I firmly believe we've unearthed a gem in Michael Jolley and I'm very confident in our future under his stewardship. We looked dead and buried a few weeks ago and are now on the cusp of securing safety. I know it's not over yet and we have some tough games coming up but I'm more confident than ever. Even if disaster happens and we went down, I'd have every confidence that MJ would get us back up a hell of a lot quicker than when we were down there previously.

BUT, that's not going to be needed as I think we'll get at least a point at home next week vs County, we can then start looking to a more successful, productive future as a football club and begin getting back to where we all believe we belong.

There's no reason why we can't be next season's Accrington, with the right backing and recruitment, anything is possible under our new manager. #UTM

The fear of relegation still wasn't banished as Barnet had matched Town's three points but the presence of Morecambe in between Town and the bottom two was a huge psychological boost. Grimsby needed one win or two draws from their last two games, to allow for Barnet picking up maximum points in theirs. Chesterfield were now all but relegated, who would have thought that would happen on the first day of the season?

Pos	Team	P	W	D	L	F	A	GD	Pts
1	Accrington	43	28	6	9	74	41	+33	90
2	Luton	44	24	12	8	91	45	+46	84
3	Wycombe	44	22	12	10	76	59	+17	78
4	Exeter	44	23	8	13	62	51	+11	77
5	Notts County	44	21	13	10	70	46	+24	76
6	Lincoln	43	19	14	10	59	44	+15	71
7	Coventry	43	21	8	14	56	42	+14	71
8	Mansfield	44	17	17	10	63	49	+14	68
9	Swindon	44	19	7	18	64	65	-1	64
10	Carlisle	44	16	15	13	59	52	+7	63
11	Colchester	44	16	13	15	53	51	+2	61
12	Cambridge	43	16	12	15	50	58	-8	60
13	Crawley Town	44	16	10	18	56	63	-7	58
14	Newport County	42	14	15	13	51	54	-3	57
15	Stevenage	44	13	13	18	57	63	-6	52
16	Cheltenham	44	13	12	19	65	65	0	51
17	Crewe	44	15	5	24	58	73	-15	50
18	Port Vale	44	11	14	19	48	60	-12	47
19	Yeovil	43	12	10	21	56	71	-15	46
20	Forest Green	43	13	7	23	53	71	-18	46
21	Grimsby	44	11	12	21	37	65	-28	45
22	Morecambe	43	9	17	17	41	55	-14	44
23	Barnet	44	10	10	24	42	65	-23	40
24	Chesterfield	43	9	8	26	45	78	-33	35

League Table 22nd April

WEEK 51

Barnet fans were bemoaning Grimsby's luck after it turned out the penalty against Swindon relied on a huge slice of fortune as the "clip" from the defender turned out to be from Cardwell's other foot. The disallowed goal also it must be said was far from clear-cut, and the Town's defenders' frantic appeals for handball certainly looked from the stands to influence the referee. There was little sympathy from the Town supporters though for their Barnet counterparts.

---

promotion plaice *As has been said on here........how many dodgy penalties has Akinde won for Barnet over recent seasons......hypocrites.*

Grimsby just needed a win against Notts County, who though, like Swindon, had everything to play for at the other end of the table.

Grimsby took the lead through Nathan Clarke in the first half, survived a few scares, but looked have blown it when Notts County equalised in the 90th minute. Amazingly though Town came back in injury time and a Grimsby striker scored from open play for the first time since September! Jamille Matt popped up in the 93rd minute to head Grimsby back in front. Town had actually gone and done it with a game to spare! Barnet had won too, so it meant Town would have needed something from the final game at Forest Green, had they not beaten County. They now could head to Gloucestershire for an end-of-season party with both clubs, once great rivals in the National League, guaranteed safety. With Chesterfield down, the final relegation place was between Barnet and Morecambe who had taken over from Grimsby as the "third team" in the equation. Grimsby amazingly were now 18th!

Hagrid *Wow! What an ending to an awful season! But wow. Some outstanding performances today from certain players, I thought Hooper and Clarke, both much maligned throughout the season were superb, my MOTM was Summerfield. Now we can all just rest. Mention to Jolley, what a job he has done sorting out Slade's mess. Phew!!!!! UTFM for next year*

ginnywings *A thoroughly deserved win. We were the better side from start to finish and if Notts County is the standard needed to get to the top of the league, it shouldn't take much to get there. Jolley has totally transformed the players and the team. The left and right sides of the pitch look far better with Fox, Hooper, RHJ and Clifton. If we had a decent striker to finish off the moves, we would have battered them. For about ten minutes, when Barnet scored and then they equalised, it looked like we were going to undeservedly miss our chance, but for once in a* blue moon a striker scored and it couldn't have been at a better time. Clarke's goal was put away like a seasoned frontman, passing the ball into the net.

I think that is the best I have seen us play for a long, long time and I'm glad we decided it for ourselves and not had to rely on others. A very rare great day at BP.

It was Michael Jolley, though, the man nobody had heard of, who the board had appointed partly from desperation, but mainly because of his aura and clear communication skills, that the fans now regarded as practically a demigod.

---

dapperz fun pub: Back him in the summer. Let him restructure the club from top to bottom, let him get rid of the dead wood throughout and build us up .. anyone who can make this lot get a few points needs full control

Pizzzza: The 12 points that we have gained under MJ have got us over the line and helped preserve our league status for next season. However, I just want to pay tribute to the man that got us the other 36 points. Where would we be without those 36 points? Relegated long ago that's where! So, while we celebrate tonight, let's all raise a glass to the unsung hero of our season... Mr Russell Slade.

forza ivano: Thank you, thank you, thank you. I am sat here in my local in the middle of nowhere getting gently pissed and with tears in my eyes as I contemplate what you have achieved. For all too rare an occasion I am wearing my Town shirt with pride. It's up there with the three Wembley finals.

The great thing is that I think you actually do understand what this means to thousands, and I mean thousands of people, whose history is wrapped up in this club from this little remote seaport with its poverty and its problems and its image problem. And you have made us proud again.

I can't write too much more cos I'm too emotional. God am I looking forward to next season. You can have got yourself a real opportunity, just be aware that when Grimsby gets behind its club and gets its momentum you will be going on a special, special ride. Thank you again. Enjoy your evening and if you ever find your way to North Marston there's a bottle of Portuguese red with your name on behind the bar

forza ivano (the following day): I still stand by those words but, Christ, am I hanging this morning :(

The league table was amazing, Town had jumped up to 18th. What was all the fuss about?!

Pos	Team	P	W	D	L	F	A	GD	Pts
1	Accrington	45	29	6	10	76	43	+33	93
2	Luton	45	25	12	8	94	46	+48	87
3	Wycombe	45	23	12	10	78	60	+18	81
4	Exeter	45	23	8	14	63	54	+9	77
5	Notts County	45	21	13	11	71	48	+23	76
6	Coventry	45	22	8	15	64	47	+17	74
7	Lincoln	45	20	14	11	63	47	+16	74
8	Mansfield	45	18	17	10	66	51	+15	71
9	Carlisle	45	17	15	13	61	53	+8	66
10	Swindon	45	19	8	18	64	65	-1	65
11	Newport County	44	16	15	13	55	56	-1	63
12	Colchester	45	16	14	15	53	51	+2	62
13	Cambridge	45	16	13	16	51	60	-9	61
14	Crawley Town	45	16	10	19	57	65	-8	58
15	Stevenage	45	14	13	18	60	64	-4	55
16	Crewe	45	16	5	24	60	74	-14	53
17	Cheltenham	45	13	12	20	66	71	-5	51
18	Grimsby	45	12	12	21	39	66	-27	48
19	Port Vale	45	11	14	20	49	62	-13	47
20	Yeovil	45	12	11	22	58	74	-16	47
21	Forest Green	45	13	8	24	54	74	-20	47
22	Morecambe	45	9	18	18	41	56	-15	45
23	Barnet	45	11	10	24	43	65	-22	43
24	Chesterfield	44	9	8	27	46	80	-34	35

League Table 29th April

Rob Sedgwick

WEEK 52

Fans spent much of the week reflecting what had happened, and for once all thoughts of the next weekend and what might happen, were pushed aside.

---

jock dock tower. *The last ten minutes of the match for me on Saturday encapsulated everything that is great about football, and Grimsby Town FC.*

Waiting anxiously for news to come through from afar that the referee had blown for full time only to suffer utter dejection and despair to realise it was now 1-1 and likely to go down to the last game of the season. Three minutes later and cue bedlam. I wasn't 250 miles then I was in a virtual BP celebrating with all the other Town fans. At the other end of the ground the County fans were going through the exact opposite emotions to ours with each turn and twist of the game. Football can be a cruel lover, but it can also be the giver of all things. I'm lucky, or unlucky as the case may be, in having watched Town for 55 years now (still a Junior in terms of others on here I know)

To enjoy the highs you have to have experienced the lows, and as a club we have had more of those than I care to remember. Relegations, re-election to the Football League back in 1969-70, abject performances in those dark faraway days of 1960's Division 4 life. Managers who took this club to the brink of disaster, and sometimes disaster itself: Mike Lyons, Mike Newell, Neil Woods (although I do not blame him personally for that) have all seen fans reaching for the anti-depressants. With those days though do come sometimes when being a Town fan can just seem extraordinarily sublime.

Lawrie McMenemy's 1971-2 Division 4 Championship season - my first of going to watch Town away regularly as I was now a wage-earner at 17. Being in huge away followings all over the UK and feeling like the Cock O the North everywhere we went. John Newman, George Kerr, David Booth and the wonderful players we had back then, many of whom were homegrown and gave you a real affinity to YOUR club. Alan Buckley. What more could possibly be said? I often hark back to the away FAC tie at Middlesborough as our finest achievement under him, when we went to a club sitting fifth in the top division and we beat them, comfortably in the end, little Grimsby Town from the bottom division. Harry Haddocks at Wimbledon, who could ever forget that? Winning at Anfield with THAT goal, winning at Everton in 1984-5 with THAT goal from Wilko, the year Everton were First Division champions. Wembley two seasons back.

It's an emotional roller coaster being a true football fan, not just at BP, but all over the UK, although we must feel it more than most, eh? Forget the prawn sandwich eating brigade, the glory hunters at Manchester City and Chelsea - I remember us gubbing City 4-0 at BP when they couldn't live with us, just as I remember us winning at Chelsea in the mid-1980s, coming back from 2-0 down at halftime to win 3-2. Anyone else remember when we sat proudly atop the old Division Two in 1982-3 after winning 4-1 away at Middlesbrough to have six wins and a draw from our opening seven games, scoring seventeen goals along the way?

It's so important to remember the bad times, the good times - for most clubs - don't exist without them. It's how you use the knowledge gained from the bad times to move onwards and upwards, and more than anything else this is my sincere hope for next season rather than falling into the same trap again. If John Fenty stays, give MJ free rein. Do not interfere. Paddy Hamilton didn't interfere with Lawrie McMenemy, and I genuinely think that if we get it right off the pitch from now until the start of next season the glory days might not be too far away as they were back then. UTFM.

Saturday came, and the transformation was complete. JJ Hooper, the man who couldn't score, the worst number 9 in the club's history, was unplayable and scored a brilliant hat-trick to beat Forest Green 3-0. It was the icing on the cake, a brilliant turnaround that was nothing short of miraculous. The team that hadn't won for half the season, that had gone 20 games without a win, and barely a point for weeks at a time, scoring only 8 goals during that spell, had finished the season with 13 points in the last 6 games. Barnet won to also pick up 13 points in 6 but because Morecambe and Coventry both got the point they needed, it was not enough from them. So, Chesterfield and Barnet, bottom two for most of the last third of the season, finally went down, and Town fans could look forward to next year.

Barralad A great day in the very hot sun. The biggest cheer before the second half started was for a six-year-old who was doing a sponsored run around the pitch for his seriously ill younger brother. Absolutely nothing happened on the pitch apart from the second biggest cheer when Mad Gav got booked.

The second half was totally different. Once Hooper's toe-poke took fully 30 seconds to cross the line there was only one team in it. Hooper's second was pretty good...the third was absolutely sublime.

Macca made his regulation two decent saves. Clark and Collins dealt with everything FGR could throw at them. Summerfield was busy as usual. Rose did his bit well.

At the end Jolley motioned to the players to come across to the fans but he made sure that we knew that he thought they'd done everything he'd asked of them. We all know that was the last we'll see of some of them but what a swansong.

I am already excited for next season.

Unfortunately, an altercation with a Grimsby supporter and John Fenty was picked up and put on Facebook.

Gaffer58: *Two things:*
1) why was he on the pitch, surely a banning order on the way, as Forest Green had already requested "fans" and that what John claims he is, to keep off the pitch to allow the players to parade round. 2) hasn't he learnt anything from the last few weeks, keep your head down and let the players/manager be the centre of attention, not the non-chairman. When Manure win the league, the Glaziers are not on the pitch trying to take the glory.

RichMariner: *I don't mind Fenty's passion and like most fans I recognise that he does want the best for this football club.*

I don't think for one minute that he's trying to ruin the club.

I do, however, wonder why he wants his loans back when true fans pay their money to watch the club - that money keeps the club afloat and helps with all manner of things. When do we ask for it back?

He won't get his loans back because he's incapable of running this football club at a profit. So, we're stuck with him for as long as he think (and wants) his benign loans back.

The biggest problem with Fenty, by far, is his ego. The guy has never accepted that he's made a mistake. Ever.

You can't tell him that he's done anything wrong. In his eyes, he's the saviour of this football club, and his absolute failure to see it any other way is his undoing.

He believes he's untouchable. He believes he's always right. The thing that threatens our future the most is John Fenty.

The board and John Fenty were still not exactly popular, but most supporters at least acknowledged the part they had played in the recovery.

Superdan147: 1/ well done on appointing Michael Jolley. Every credit

2/ No excuses now, next week get this man on a long-term contract. No 6-month rolling contracts. The turnaround has been remarkable. The way he has conducted himself has been exemplary. Every single Grimsby Town fan is excited, overjoyed and amazed at the job he has done and what we can achieve under him. PLEASE get this man tied up on a long-term deal (Cambridge and Lincoln amongst others have just tied up their managers on long-term deals) we simply have to do the same.

3/ Give Him FULL support and total control. Whatever decisions he makes, support them. Whatever he needs (give him it) with his background I'm sure he won't leave us in a poor financial state.

This could be the start of a golden era for GTFC. TIME TO ACT

Regards

Every Grimsby Town fan UTM

GyFerrers: In some way I feel sorry for him. I don't think he's deliberately tried to ruin the club. He is a fan and whether I agree with the benign loan scenario or not, he put his cash on the line.

I just wish he'd learn, be a fan and enjoy the ride. When it gets lumpy stay quiet, when it goes well praise the Manager and fans. When it goes really well sit back and have a deep sense of fan satisfaction.

You've made a lot of mistakes John, so have I and so has everyone. Whether the club would or wouldn't still exist without you is irrelevant. Please, for your own sanity stay in the background.

GrimRob: The most important thing is to keep MJ here and give him stability. Players are less likely to come to a club in turmoil with no recognised leader. We need to persuade 20 young men to come here and further their careers. Unless a benefactor of means can be found then I'd choose JF over turmoil any day. Yes, it would be nice if he put a bit more money in the pot next season, maybe he will, I am sure he's pondering what to do next by way of a statement.

JF soon issued a rather sheepish statement explaining how the altercation with the fan had come about and promising to investigate a membership scheme for exiled supporters which he had discussed with some friendlier fans at the game.

Link:https://www.grimsby-townfc.co.uk/news/2018/may/a-message-to-our-supporters-moving-forward-together-stronger/

SteffiMariner. Well, that'll out the Fishy in a meltdown. Quite a good statement in my eyes. PR appears to be improving alongside results...

Meanwhile the club immediately issued season tickets for next season, capitalising on the feel-good factor.

Heppy88. Great forward planning to sell season tickets this early in the season. I always believed it would have been a good idea after winning promotion, but never happened. So great to see the club capitalise on the staying up/Jolley feel-good factor.

So just been to renew with my Mum. Nothing was too much problem and the season tickets were ready for collection!

I was told a few had already been in to renew and about £4000 of sales already on the internet.

You can't help but sense there are positive changes at the club other than those on the pitch and even the staff appear more relaxed and generally happier. So credit where credit is due. UTMM!!

The big debate on who to get rid of started immediately. Many of the players who a few weeks ago had seemed certainties to be shown the door, fans were starting to have second thoughts about and even Siriki Dembele, who once looked the best player at the club, was a question mark after over half a season with persistent injury problems.

Horsforthmariner. The posts on Dembele are ridiculous. Of course, we should keep him. Loads of kids burst onto the scene but struggle towards the end of their first season. It's tiredness and the body takes time to get used to the battering it takes as a pro. He'll learn and come on better next season.

Pos	Team	P	W	D	L	F	A	GD	Pts
1	Accrington	46	29	6	11	76	46	+30	93
2	Luton	46	25	13	8	94	46	+48	88
3	Wycombe	46	24	12	10	79	60	+19	84
4	Exeter	46	24	8	14	64	54	+10	80
5	Notts County	46	21	14	11	71	48	+23	77
6	Coventry	46	22	9	15	64	47	+17	75
7	Lincoln	46	20	15	11	64	48	+16	75
8	Mansfield	46	18	18	10	67	52	+15	72
9	Swindon	46	20	8	18	67	65	+2	68
10	Carlisle	46	17	16	13	62	54	+8	67
11	Newport County	46	16	16	14	56	58	-2	64
12	Cambridge	46	17	13	16	56	60	-4	64
13	Colchester	46	16	14	16	53	52	+1	62
14	Crawley Town	46	16	11	19	58	66	-8	59
15	Crewe	46	17	5	24	62	75	-13	56
16	Stevenage	46	14	13	19	60	65	-5	55
17	Cheltenham	46	13	12	21	67	73	-6	51
18	Grimsby	46	13	12	21	42	66	-24	51
19	Yeovil	46	12	12	22	59	75	-16	48
20	Port Vale	46	11	14	21	49	67	-18	47
21	Forest Green	46	13	8	25	54	77	-23	47
22	Morecambe	46	9	19	18	41	56	-15	46
23	Barnet	46	12	10	24	46	65	-19	46
24	Chesterfield	46	10	8	28	47	83	-36	38

Final League Table

The league position over the 2017-2018 season followed a very similar pattern to the previous campaign for the first half, threatening but never challenging the top 7. The 20-match winless run saw a steep fall in position, but the late run saw Town pull away from the danger zone in style.

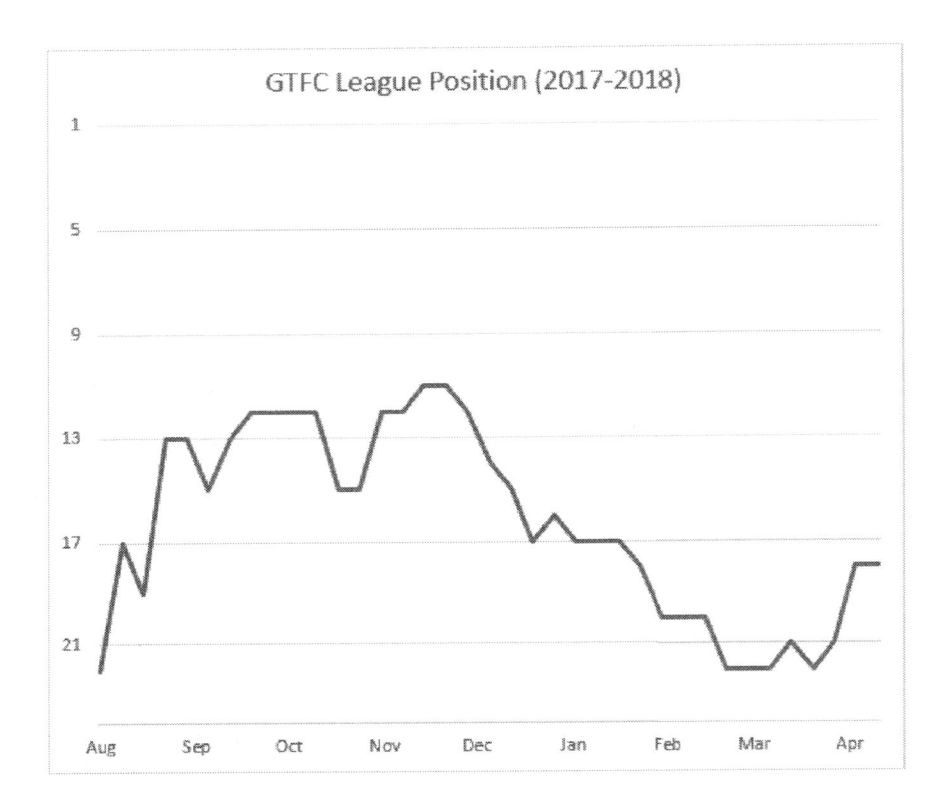

2017 -2018 Week by Week

CONCLUSIONS

What is apparent from this narrative is how often fans overreact. Many supporters greeted a run of two or three wins as a signal of an impending assault on the league. Likewise, dozens of supporters were resigned to relegation, even though Grimsby were never in the bottom two places and at no stage did the bookmakers deem them one of the two most likely teams to go down. I think it's no exaggeration though to say that Michael Jolley rescued the season, had Russell Slade been kept in charge results might have improved a bit, but not to the extent that they did under the new boss.

Games at Blundell Park, until the last three, were dire. Even with those games considered Grimsby had the worst home record in League Two. Entertainment was lacking, and positive results about as rare as a striker's goal. There can be few years when the paying public have experienced so little entertainment as this one. Fortunately for season ticket sales, the best games were the last three, so the memories of all those turgid matches may be buried under happier memories for a lot of fans, and the chief architect of the misery, Russell Slade, has of course long left, followed in the summer by his not so able assistant Paul Wilkinson. There is every reason to believe that entertainment and at least a few more wins might be part of the Saturday afternoon experience in Cleethorpes in the next 12 months.

The board, and John Fenty in particular, came under a huge amount of criticism. Some of it was deserved, and they didn't help themselves on numerous occasions. Their harshest critics will never change their spots, but more moderate supporters joined them during the period covered by this book. The moderates can probably be won back but it will take time. The decision to bring back Russell Slade, never a popular choice amongst supporters, almost disastrously backfired. But the board are capable of good appointments too, as the six years under Paul Hurst bear testimony to, but Michael Jolley in comparison has proved to be a rabbit plucked from a hat. Rob Scott and Paul Hurst were managing nearby Boston, so were a fairly obvious target to approach. Jolley, in contrast, had just managed a team who had been relegated from the Swedish Allsvenskan, an outpost of football, and was all but unheard of to most British football fans apart from the more informed followers of the teams in this country where he had previously worked. It was a big gamble taking on Jolley under the circumstances, but the board deserve credit for their bravery in doing so.

Clearly there is a divide between many of the supporters, especially those who use social media, and the board. Only time will tell, but the best way to heal that impasse is success on the pitch, and for a few joyous games at the end of 2017-2018, we experienced it and can savour the memories until football begins in earnest again.

I make no predictions where the future will take Grimsby Town FC.

UTM

Rob Sedgwick
June 2018

AFTERMATH

Most of the team departed but more players were retained than looked likely when Michael Jolley took over. There will be a lot of new faces next season, but some of the previous season's squad will be welcomed back, not quite as heroes but certainly with expectations of better things.

Player of the Season: James McKeown
Young Player of the Season: Harry Clifton
Goal of the Season: JJ Hooper (3rd goal vs Forest Green)
Players Released: Ben Davies, Nathan Clarke, James Berrett, Tom Sawyer, Jack Keeble, Ben Killip, Scott Vernon, Karleigh Osborne, Gary McSheffrey, Sean McAllister, Zak Mills, Chris Clements
Loan players departed: Jamille Matt, Jake Kean, Simeon Jackson, Easah Suliman, Diallang Jaiyesimi, Mallik Wilks, Charles Vernam
Players offered new contracts: James McKeown, Luke Summerfield, Martyn Woolford, Danny Collins, Andrew Fox, Ahkeem Rose
Players already under contract: Paul Dixon, Mitch Rose, JJ Hooper, Sam Kelly, Harry Cardwell

The board and John Fenty remained in charge of the club. Michael Jolley remained as manager, but Assistant Manager Paul Wilkinson was released.

Rob Sedgwick

ACKNOWLEDGEMENTS

Thanks to all the hundreds of people who posted on the Fishy during the season. Many different people contributed to this book, but many other posts could equally have been chosen for publication. The forum really is the sum of the parts, not just a few choice posts as I have assembled in this narrative.

Thanks to the fans for giving us all something to talk about. They are the ones who ultimately drive the whole business of football, turning up week after week in the (fairly unlikely) hope of going home happier than when they set off.

Thanks to the Grimsby Town players, managers, club staff and board members. You do sometimes get a hard time from the forum members on occasions, but the arduous work you all put in is also appreciated too.

Thanks to the forum moderators for keeping an eye on proceedings and the occasional need to intervene due to an "overenthusiastic" poster.

Thanks to those who have checked earlier versions of this manuscript and spotted the factual mistakes and typos: Trevor Hewson, Leon Harding, Nana Amoafo, Robin White and Pauline Hetherington.

If you notice a mistake of any kind, or you have any comments (good or bad) drop me a line at rob@thefishy.co.uk. I'd love to hear from you.

Printed in Great Britain
by Amazon